AN ESSENTIAL GUIDE TO

baptism
in the
holy spirit

D0483839

AN ESSENTIAL GUIDE TO

baptism
in the
holy spirit

Ron Phillips

CHARISMA
HOUSE

Most CHARISMA HOUSE BOOK GROUP products are available at special quantity discounts for bulk purchase for sales promotions, premiums, fund-raising, and educational needs. For details, write Charisma House Book Group, 600 Rinehart Road, Lake Mary, Florida 32746, or telephone (407) 333-0600.

AN ESSENTIAL GUIDE TO BAPTISM IN THE HOLY SPIRIT by
    Ron Phillips
Published by Charisma House
Charisma Media/Charisma House Book Group
600 Rinehart Road
Lake Mary, Florida 32746
www.charismahouse.com

This book or parts thereof may not be reproduced in any form, stored in a retrieval system, or transmitted in any form by any means—electronic, mechanical, photocopy, recording, or otherwise—without prior written permission of the publisher, except as provided by United States of America copyright law.

Unless otherwise noted, all Scripture quotations are from the New King James Version of the Bible. Copyright © 1979, 1980, 1982 by Thomas Nelson, Inc., publishers. Used by permission.

Scripture quotations marked CEV are from the Contemporary English Version, copyright © 1995 by the American Bible Society. Used by permission.

Scripture quotations marked KJV are from the King James Version of the Bible.

Scripture quotations marked NIV are from the Holy Bible, New International Version. Copyright © 1973, 1978, 1984, International Bible Society. Used by permission.

Scripture quotations marked TLB are from The Living Bible. Copyright © 1971. Used by permission of Tyndale House Publishers, Inc., Wheaton, IL 60189. All rights reserved.

Cover design by Justin Evans
Design Director: Bill Johnson

Copyright © 2011 by Ron Phillips
All rights reserved

Visit the author's website at www.ronphillips.org.

Library of Congress Cataloging-in-Publication Data:
Phillips, Ron M.
  An essential guide to baptism in the Holy Spirit / Ron Phillips. --
1st ed.
       p. cm.
  Includes bibliographical references.
  ISBN 978-1-61638-239-1 (trade paper) -- ISBN
978-1-61638-421-0
(e-book) 1. Baptism in the Holy Spirit. I. Title.
  BT123.P47 2011
  234'.13--dc22

                          2011002444

This publication is translated in Spanish under the title *Una guía esencial para el bautismo en el Espíritu Santo*, copyright © 2011 by Ron Phillips, published by Casa Creación, a Charisma Media company. All rights reserved.

12 13 14 15 — 9 8 7 6 5 4 3
Printed in the United States of America

CONTENTS

CHAPTER ONE
My Own Story

As my plane sped westward toward a speaking engagement, I felt that my life as I had known it for twenty-two years had come to an end. At age forty-two, the dew of my youth had long since dried up. I had reached what would be considered by many to be the pinnacle of evangelical life. I served a large and growing congregation of Christians. My family was intact and devoted. How could I have felt so inadequate and miserable? These thoughts tumbled over and over in my mind. I fumblingly opened my laptop and began to write out my resignation to the ministry. As the twenty-six years of my education, vocation, and calling began to evaporate before my eyes, my mind reflected on the years of my life.

I remembered the deep conviction of the Holy Spirit on my life at the age of eight. The fires of revival and harvest swept through Montgomery, Alabama. Our young church met in a tent for weeks. A powerful evangelist named C. E. Autrey preached at these meetings, and the fire of God fell for two weeks. I trembled and wept with conviction at every gathering of the church.

Finally, my pastor, John Bob Riddle, spoke to me in the front seat of his car on a late summer afternoon. Although I was too shy to pray in front of my pastor, after he drove away I bowed on my knees beside a swing set in my backyard and prayed for Jesus to save me. I remember flopping down onto the grass afterward and gazing up into the stars; I felt as though I were floating right through them.

At age fourteen, I felt God tugging at my heart with a call to preach. At the time, I resisted His gentle prodding because I feared the prospect of speaking in front of others. God continued His work in my heart, however, and when I was sixteen years old, I ran down an aisle at a youth revival, yielding my life to His service. I was so overcome with emotion and tears there at the altar that the minister couldn't understand my incoherent confession of my decision. When others told him later of my call to preach, this godly man wasted no time in giving me a preaching assignment in a service.

Thus my spiritual life had begun with an overwhelming conversion experience and a fiery call to the ministry. It was a natural step at the age of eighteen to further my training at Clarke College, a Baptist institution in Newton, Mississippi. There I gained a number of friends who loved to speak of spiritual things and the power of the Holy Spirit. During a school break, I journeyed to Camp Zion in Myrtle, Mississippi, where I first felt the longing for more of God. This was the first time I ever heard a Baptist explain outward works.

Later that year I was invited to speak at a weekend youth revival in Natchez, Mississippi. I failed miserably in my preaching effort on Friday evening, preaching every sermon I had in the course of twenty minutes! Early the next morning a pastor took me in a back room and asked me if I had ever been filled with the Holy Spirit. I confessed that I had not, and, in fact, I didn't know what he was talking about. He laid his hands on me and prayed, and I felt a surge of power rush through me. I preached with a greater anointing the rest of the weekend. I learned that preaching only with your mind and intellect was not sufficient.

I left those early experiences behind and went on to Samford University at age nineteen. While a student, I became a pastor of a small church. A year later, Paulette and I were married, and our lives were caught up in an unceasing succession of school and church activities that went on for seven years.

In 1974, I received my doctorate of ministry from New Orleans Baptist Theological Seminary. With my degree, a wife, and the addition of two precious daughters, we moved to minister in Alabama. In the next five years I consecutively pastored two churches, seeing both ministries complete building and remodeling projects as the attendance thrived.

In 1979, I was called to pastor at Central Baptist Church in Hixson, Tennessee, where I currently serve, and the Lord continued to bless. My family soon expanded with the addition of a son. We began radio and TV ministries, broke records in church giving and attendance, and completed several new building projects.

The years of ministry brought me much success in religious life. However, I felt burned out instead of on fire for God. I knew how to play the game, draw a crowd, and stay in favor with denominational leadership. Yet personally I was miserable.

What had happened to my first love? Where had the passion to preach gone? Where was the joy of ministry?

Back on that airplane, I finished typing a one-page resignation letter just as we touched down in Albuquerque. I would complete this speaking assignment, return to my church, and quit!

Upon my arrival at the conference center, I found my room and then made my way to hear the evening speaker, Mrs. Minette Drumwright. Since my assignment to speak was not until the next morning, I sat in the back so I could make an easy exit if the session proved to be boring. After all, in my fundamentalist world, women were not to have much to say.

Was I in for a surprise!

Mrs. Drumwright began to share about the tragic and untimely death of her husband, Huber, who had been a minister and denominational executive. His sudden death had brought her face-to-face with her own spiritual needs. She confessed that her husband had been her spiritual support, and at his death, she felt as though her spiritual foundation had been suddenly kicked out from under her. She announced that it was a fresh filling of the Holy Spirit and a new walk with the Lord that had sustained her.

Such words were not new to me. I had read *The Key to Triumphant Living* by Jack Taylor.[1] I had read R. A. Torrey's testimony on the baptism of the Holy Spirit. At a previous state conference I had heard Stephen Olford's eloquent call to the Spirit-filled life. Across the years, I had, in fact, experienced temporary touches of the power of God. Yet I refused to believe in a "second blessing." I reasoned that the Holy Spirit stuff was for the Charismatics. I was an educated pastor who could read the Greek New Testament!

Despite those thoughts, I undeniably felt all of my prejudice melt away as I tearfully left that hall for my room. I fell exhausted across my bed and slumbered into a fitful sleep.

In the night I heard my name being called. The voice was deep and clear. Going to the door, I found no one there. I returned to my sleep, but I was certain that I had heard my name called. Before long I heard my name called again. Startled, I got up and looked down the hall and out the window. No one seemed to be there.

As I was awakened a third time, my room was filled with God's presence. It was the voice of my dear Savior. I wept as the glory filled the room, and I cried out, "Lord, where have You been?"

He said to me, "I have been waiting for you."

I asked, "Lord, where have You been waiting?"

He replied, "Read your scripture for today."

It was my discipline to read five psalms a day, and since it was the nineteenth day of the month, I opened my Bible to Psalm 91 and read these assuring words:

> He who dwells in the secret place of the Most High
> Shall abide under the shadow of the Almighty.
> I will say of the Lord, "He is my refuge and my
> fortress;
> My God, in Him I will trust."
>
> —Psalm 91:1–2

A secret place! Why had I never seen this? *How* had I never realized this? The "Most High" had a secret place, an intimate place where I could meet Him and receive power. Not only did this place exist, but also my heavenly Father longed for me to enter in and commune with Him. I read on to discover that I could be anointed with fresh oil.

> But my horn You have exalted like a wild ox;
> I have been anointed with fresh oil.
>
> —Psalm 92:10

Soon His presence and anointing overcame me. Fresh oil and new wine poured into my dry and thirsty soul. It was the baptism of power. I wept, sang, laughed, shouted, shook, and lay at peace before Him. I left that place never to be the same. I had moved into a new realm of communication and power with God. A fire burned in my soul that rages until this very day. A burning passion for Jesus and a desire to do His will came upon my life.

Did I speak with tongues right away? Though I did not understand this gift, I woke up several times with a new language on my tongue. The full manifestation and understanding of that gift would come later.

Initial Difficulties

A few months later, my dad died unexpectedly. Just as many in bereavement have come to realize, I knew there were things that I wished I could have said to him, and I was in grief that I did not get to say good-bye.

Then came the blow of all blows; an associate pastor was arrested. His actions generated a storm of bad publicity for the ministry. Members as well as non-members called my integrity into question. It was a dark moment.

One evening in the midst of this crisis, my heart seemed to stop, and I fainted. Rushed to the hospital, I was told that I had a "heart incident." Later that evening someone came into the room and prayed over me for my healing. My heart was found to be undamaged, and God restored my health, but the close call took its toll on my hurting spirit.

Another associate suffered a heart attack. Thankfully he recovered and continued serving God with fresh anointing. In spite of the crisis confronting our church, I watched and rejoiced as I saw God direct Spirit-filled men and women to join our staff, each one bringing fresh enthusiasm and specific giftings that enabled the church ministry to expand.

While skeptics predicted our church would likely go to pieces, the very opposite proved to be true. The church grew at a rate of two for every one who left. Questions and discussion concerning the crisis were handled privately so that church business and worship were never hindered. The staff and deacons were trusted to take care of these problems.[2]

Many more of our people began to move in the power of the Holy Spirit. In the midst of a staff prayer meeting in fall of 1992, God spoke clearly that He would grow the church if we would allow Him to do a "new thing." This word was based on these verses from Isaiah:

> When you pass through the waters, I will be with you; and through the rivers, they shall not overflow you. When you walk through the fire, you shall not be burned, nor shall the flame scorch you....Behold, I will do a new thing....For I will pour water on him who is thirsty, and floods on the dry ground; I will pour My Spirit on your descendants, and My blessing on your offspring;...No weapon formed against you shall prosper.
> —ISAIAH 43:2; 44:3; 54:17

The power of God fell in that room, and we left there with the assurance that all would be well with the body.

More than two decades have passed since those days, and our church has continued to surge in revival power, though the storms have come frequently.

Revival at Last

As awakening broke out in our church, and wave after wave of blessing has flowed ever since. Membership, attendance, and finances have more than doubled, even though hundreds have left who were fearful of the move of God! The church's ministry is worldwide via television, radio, and printed media. Thousands are walking in fullness and freedom today.

All of the distinct signs of revival have followed, bringing the church under scrutiny and criticism. People have been saved, healed, and delivered from demons. They have trembled, wept, laughed, shouted, and fallen in the Spirit. Praise and worship, including singing, clapping, hand raising, body movement, and spiritual singing, continue to mark the services.

Are these experiences valid? Is what is happening biblically accurate? Did these signs happen in church history? The following chapters will give biblical and historical evidence for the baptism of the Holy Spirit.

CHAPTER TWO
An Old Testament Promise

RESSED IN LEATHER and with his breath smelling of locusts and wild honey, there burst on to the scene a prophet of God; John the Baptist appeared in the first century as the last of the prophets of the old covenant.

John, the cousin of our Lord Jesus, was born to Zacharias and Elizabeth when they were passed age (Luke 1:36). The young virgin Mary, pregnant by the Holy Ghost, journeyed to visit with her cousin Elizabeth. Upon entering the home of Elizabeth, the Holy Ghost manifested. Elizabeth was filled with the Holy Ghost and released a blessing on Mary and the unborn Jesus (Luke 1:41–42). Luke tells us in verse 40 that John the Baptist also leaped in the womb of his Holy Ghost–filled mother! Elizabeth continued to prophesy, and Mary was filled with the Holy Ghost and began to sing in the Spirit (vv. 46–55). After the birth of John, his father was filled with the Holy Ghost and prophesied (vv. 67–79). All of this happened, of course, prior to the birth of Jesus!

John the Baptist was born and reared in an atmosphere saturated with the Holy Spirit. He came in the spirit of Elijah as the promised forerunner of Israel's Messiah and the world's Savior, Jesus Christ. It is interesting that John, a man of the Spirit, "did no miracle" (John 10:41, KJV). God's prophet of Spirit baptism was never released to perform miracles.

All of this is important because John's last prophecy included the last promise from the old covenant concerning the baptism of the Holy Spirit: "John answered, saying to all, 'I indeed baptize you with water; but One mightier than I is coming, whose sandal strap I am not worthy to loose. He will baptize you with the Holy Spirit and fire'" (Luke 3:16). John's last prophecy was the promise of the baptism with the Holy Spirit and fire. It is heartrending to see how most Christians embrace the evangelical promises of John 3:16, which speaks of God's sacrificial love for us, but so few have accepted or are even familiar with the power found in the promise of Luke 3:16!

John's voice echoes a promise that resonates throughout the Old Testament. Over and over we read that the Holy Spirit came for and departed from God's people. In the Old Testament the Holy Spirit was available to save, but His abiding presence was not yet given to all.

Jesus came to die on the cross and be raised from the dead for the salvation of all who believe. The coming of the Messiah heralded the age of the Spirit, and it was through Christ's death and resurrection that the Holy Spirit was released to live in us in a way mankind had never imagined. His coming also birthed a new humanity. A second Adam had come as regent of a new kingdom, head of a new race of people, and Lord of a new entity called the church. This church, this "chosen generation" and "royal priesthood," were more than "new creatures in Christ." They were to be a people full of and empowered by the Holy Spirit!

The age of the Spirit had come as promised by the prophets. Joel 2:28 declares, "And it shall come to pass afterward that I will pour out My Spirit on all flesh." Isaiah promised that the dark days of oppression would be broken. Hear Isaiah's promise: "Until the Spirit is poured upon us from on high" (Isa. 32:15). Furthermore, Isaiah promised "a new thing" that will transition the world (Isa. 43:19). He then identified that "new thing" as the outpouring of the Holy Spirit:

> For I will pour water on him who is thirsty,
> And floods on the dry ground;
> I will pour My Spirit on your descendants,
> And My blessing on your offspring.
>   —Isaiah 44:3

The prophetic voice of the Old Testament promised both the Savior and the Spirit. When Jesus died on the cross, there came from His side water and blood, the elements of birth. The blood speaks of the new birth available to every believer, and the water speaks of the Spirit-empowered Word of God that birthed the church.

At Christ's death the veil of the temple was torn in two from top to bottom, and resurrected believers were seen after Christ's resurrection (Matt. 27:50–53). The barrier between the spiritual and earthly realms had been breached, and now the Holy Spirit could come and abide. What a colossal moment as the spiritual kingdom invades the earth!

Fifty days later during the feast of Pentecost, the disciples were gathered in the upper room. There were one hundred twenty counted for that service. Imagine that moment. The disciples and other followers had, in obedience to Jesus's command and in the hope of His promise, gone to a tiny upper room there in Jerusalem. Was it the same room that they had used as a hiding place after Jesus's death? We don't know, but we do know that these were not the same men and women— yes, women were present—who hid in fear those two nights in Jerusalem. These were a transformed people. Some might say that the transformation was yet to come, but read what the Bible tells us: These people were all a dither after the crucifixion. Peter even suggested that they go back to being fishermen. But there in the upper room were a changed people. They were all of one mind and "with one accord" when the rivers of prophecy rushed together (Acts 2:1). The room filled with the sound of a mighty rushing wind, and tongues of fire rested over the heads of all present—and the promised baptism of the Holy Spirit became available to all believers.

Jesus had promised this mighty baptism to those who obeyed Him. Acts 1:5–8 states:

> [Jesus said,] "For John truly baptized with water, but you shall be baptized with the Holy Spirit not many days from now." Therefore, when they had come together, they asked Him, saying, "Lord, will You at this time restore the kingdom to Israel?" And He said to them, "It is not for you to know times or seasons which the Father has put in His own authority. But you shall receive power when the Holy Spirit has come upon you; and you shall be witnesses to Me in Jerusalem, and in all Judea and Samaria, and to the end of the earth."

The scripture records that dramatic moment with these manifestations—a howling wind, tongues of fire, the filling of the Spirit, and speaking in tongues. Three thousand were saved in thirty minutes, and the church was birthed in charismatic glory!

Pentecost does not need to be repeated, just simply received. Jesus is now glorified and the baptism of the Holy Spirit is available to all. May the rest of this book instruct and inspire you to embrace all that God has promised!

CHAPTER THREE
Entering the Spiritual World

AT ONE TIME in our history, many considered the earth to be at the very center of God's creation, with every other created thing somehow revolving around us. Even now, our planet's twenty-five-thousand-mile circumference seems large to us, but consider these facts about our solar system:

+ Our sun is a main sequence G2 star that contains 99.86 percent of ALL the mass in our solar system.[1]

+ The combined mass of Jupiter and Saturn make up 90 percent of all the remaining mass.[2]

+ The edge of our solar system, while not precisely defined, is about 90–120 astronomical units (AU) from the sun.[3] Considering that an astronomical unit is approximately 93,000,000 miles,[4] it's at least 8,370,000,000 miles to the edge of our solar system!

Now consider some facts about our own planet.

+ The distance of the earth from the sun, its orbital eccentricity, rotational rate, axial tilt, geological history, atmospheric composition, and protective magnetic field all contribute to the conditions necessary to sustain life on this planet.[5]

- Earth's atmosphere extends out to 10,000 kilometers.[6]
- Earth has a surface area of 196,935,000 square miles.[7]
- Earth travels through space at 67,000 miles per hour.[8]

As the first, and only, inhabited planet in our solar system, we are a mind-boggling ninety-three million miles from our sun.[9] Our solar system of a sun and planets is a small part of one galaxy called the Milky Way. Our galaxy is one of at least one hundred billion galaxies,[10] but the closest star to our solar system is approximately 4.2 light-years away.[11] The vast dimensions of the created order have shattered ancient concepts of the heavenly realm. David was ahead of his time when he asked in Psalm 8:

> When I consider your heavens,
> the work of your fingers,
> the moon and the stars,
> which you have set in place,
> what is man that you are mindful of him?
>
> —PSALM 8:3–4, NIV

This means our earth is insignificant, a speck of dust in the vast universe, unless there is a creator God! Believing there is a God, we believe that He exists without the limitation of our three-dimensional world. He lives in what science calls a universal parallel to our universe, and even this is, more than anything, our best guess at understanding. All of created order that we know is only the edges of God's world. Quantum physics speak of eleven dimensions, yet God is not limited by time or space!

What Is the Spiritual World?

In order to understand the dynamics of the baptism of the Spirit, we must, as best we can, learn all we can about the spiritual world. Consider the terms *spiritual realm*, *spirit world*, and *spiritual world*. The very essence of these terms evoke images of wispy clouds, souls that are somehow glowing ethereal echoes of their physical counterparts, angels that float from cloud to cloud while playing harps, and a constant high-pitched hum that distinguishes that realm from this one. The truth that must be embraced by one attempting to understand the spiritual world is this: that realm is *more real* than this one. We must remember that this earth, this solar system, even the very galaxy is subject to God's judgment, and according to 2 Peter 3:10 (NIV):

> The heavens will disappear with a roar; the elements will be destroyed by fire, and the earth and everything in it will be laid bare.

Yes, this earth and all that we know as "real" can be wiped away, but the spiritual world is eternal and everlasting.

In the New Testament, the spiritual world was more than a home in heaven when one dies. The spiritual world is viewed in the New Testament as a present reality available to all believers who embrace the work of the Holy Spirit. As we turn the pages of the New Testament, we come to understand that humanity originates in another realm and has a destiny beyond this earth.

Listen to some of the language of the New Testament. In 1 Corinthians 2:6–16, Paul speaks of wisdom and truth flowing out of the spiritual dimension into our present world. These wonderful revelations can only be received by an individual whose human spirit has been made alive by the baptism of the Holy Spirit (1 Cor. 2:6–11). Believers can be taught by the Holy Spirit (1 Cor. 2:13). Special gifts are given by the Holy Spirit (1 Cor. 2:12).

In his natural normal life, a human being cannot receive the "things of the Spirit of God" (1 Cor. 2:14). A person must have their "normal" way of thinking taken over by the Holy Spirit. Thus "the mind of Christ," indeed a new way of thinking, can take over the life of the believer!

In Ephesians 2:5–6 the spiritual world is referred to as "the heavenly places." These verses indicate that we who are alive in Christ have access to that realm. This is the realm where Christ is enthroned right now (Eph. 1:20). At the "right hand" of the Father, Jesus intercedes for us, as does the Holy Spirit (Rom. 8:26, 34). This realm of the Spirit is where true worship occurs and also where spiritual warfare brings victory (Eph. 6:12). It is in this realm that the impossible becomes possible!

Possibly the greatest revelation about God and His desire for our lives rests in the promise found in Ephesians 3:20–21. It's here that we are told that God desires to do *more than we think or ask*. What makes the power of heaven available to those of us on Earth? The answer is the unfettered work of the Holy Spirit.

Entering the Spiritual World

How does one enter the spiritual world? A Jewish leader made that inquiry of Jesus early in His ministry. Jesus replied to him, "Most assuredly I say to you, unless one is born again, he cannot see the kingdom of God" (John 3:3). The word translated "again" is the Greek *anothen*. It can mean "above." Jesus told Nicodemus that nothing less than a new beginning, a new life, birthed *from above* could grant access to the spiritual kingdom.

Later Jesus would teach him that this new birth would come when one embraces the promises of the gospel. Salvation is a miracle work of the Holy Spirit. The Lord enters one's life at conversion. The Holy Spirit is God on the earth right now! He becomes resident and indwells every true believer.

Thus the potential of operating in all the gifts and graces of the Spirit is available to every believer. Jesus would identify this potential as a rushing artesian spring that is potentially a river of life for spiritual resources (John 4:14; 7:37–38).

It would be good to ask yourself right now, "Am I truly born from above?" It isn't as difficult a question as some would have you believe. The Philippian jailer asked what the conditions were for salvation and was told, quite simply, "Believe on the Lord Jesus Christ, and you will be saved" (Acts 16:31). It is simple acceptance of Christ's gift and belief that He did *all* the work necessary for your salvation. If you have never recognized this and accepted His gift, why don't you pray this prayer?

> *Lord Jesus, I confess my own failures and faults. I believe You were given to die for my sins on the cross. I believe You rose from the dead and are alive right now and hearing my prayer. Please come into my life and save me. Give me the birth from above and a brand-new life. You are Lord! Amen.*

If you prayed that and meant it with your whole heart, the kingdom of the Spirit and access to that *more real* spiritual world is now available to you.

> They were in an upper chamber,
> They were all with one accord,

When the Holy Ghost descended
As was promised by the Lord.
Yes, the power from heav'n descended
With the sound of rushing wind;
Tongues of fire came down upon them,
As the Lord said He would send.
Yes, this "old time" power was given
To our fathers who were true;
This is promised to believers,
And we all may have it too.[12]

CHAPTER FOUR
The Seal of God

FOLLOWING THE NEW birth by the Spirit into the kingdom of God, there is a second work. That second work, the *need* in the believer's life, is the baptism of the Holy Spirit. The baptism of the Holy Spirit is part of the work of Jesus Christ in your life. John said that Jesus is the baptizer in the Holy Spirit (Luke 3:16). You must desire all that Jesus has for you in order to embrace this promise.

While the Holy Spirit indwells our lives after conversion, the baptism of the Holy Spirit allows what is on the inside to move out of our lives. The word *baptism* means to be immersed. Thus, a believer has the Holy Spirit that was "in him" now "upon him." With all that we discuss in our Christian circles about various baptisms (and we truly only touch the tip of a substantial iceberg), it is easy to understand that there exists some confusion about the doctrine of baptisms.

Is There One Baptism?

Just the mention of the baptism of the Holy Spirit causes hackles to rise on most of my contemporaries. The traditional view is that the baptism of the Holy Spirit is what Paul mentioned in 1 Corinthians 12:13:

> For by one Spirit we were all baptized into one body—whether Jews or Greeks, whether slaves or free—and have all been made to drink into one Spirit.

Ephesians 4 is cited to make the argument for only one baptism in the believer's life. This passage refers to "one Lord, one faith, one baptism." Thus, opponents of God's work conclude, "You see, all of this talk of a baptism of the Spirit following conversion is foolish." They then want to disclaim what they call a second work of grace. But what does the Bible say in its accounts of the lives of New Testament believers? Are there groups that were clearly saved, even to the point of water baptism, but had not yet received the Spirit baptism?

In Acts 6:5, when the apostles chose Stephen to lead the men selected to give pastoral care to the widows, he was described as one who "had great faith and was filled with the Holy Spirit" (CEV). It seems, then, that a believer being "filled" held a special significance to the apostles. Watch the progression found in the eighth chapter of Acts. There we are told that the apostles in Jerusalem had heard that there were some people in Samaria who had "accepted God's message," so they (the apostles) sent Peter and John (Acts 8:14, CEV). When these two mighty apostles from Jesus's inner circle arrived, they prayed with the knowledge that the people in Samaria were already believers, that those same brothers and sisters would be given the Holy Spirit, "for as yet He had fallen upon none of them. They had only been baptized in the name of the Lord Jesus." Then, when Peter and John laid hands on these baptized believers, "they received the Holy Spirit" (vv. 15–17).

In Acts 19, Paul discovered another group that had taken part in John's water baptism but were not fully informed about Jesus. He declared the truth to them, and they were baptized in the name of Jesus. It appears that in Ephesus some people were teaching two water baptisms, one to recall John the Baptist and one to be performed in obedience to Jesus. Paul taught that only one water baptism was needed, and that should take place after conversion.

A Fresh Start

Hebrews 6:2 speaks of "the doctrine of baptisms." Notice it is plural. At least three baptisms belong to every believer: positional, pictorial, and powerful.

As noted earlier, Paul stated, "For by one Spirit we were all baptized into one body" (1 Cor. 12:13). This speaks of positional baptism, wherein we are moved from one place to another, from our place as one willfully separated from God into our place as children of God. The Holy Spirit places a person into the church, the body of Christ. This is a once-and-for-all act whereby the Spirit unites the individual to the body of Christ.

I remember my own baptism vividly. I can almost remember the clothes I wore afterward during the church service. However, I can vividly recall the words spoken to me and over me during this event. I was asked to state my confession—Jesus Christ is my Lord and my Savior—and these words were spoken over me: "And because of your confession of faith, it is my privilege to baptize you, my brother, in the name of the Father, the Son, and the Holy Spirit." Then the pastor said these words—words whose full mystery were not clear to me then and are still marvelous to me now. He said, as I was lowered into the water, "You are buried with Christ in baptism unto death..." Then, as he lifted me out of the water, he said, "...and raised to walk in newness of life." Many have asked why this is important or if it is important at all. Some have greatly misconstrued the purpose of this baptism. One young believer in Christ said to me that because she had sinned since she was baptized, she needed to get baptized *again* so that she would still be saved!

Let's be clear: this pictorial baptism performs no salvific work! It is a symbolic event that is an outward and public statement of an inner working. It portrays the death, burial, and resurrection of Christ, and it identifies the believer publicly with Christ. There is only one water baptism as taught in Ephesians 4, and it is by immersion subsequent to salvation.

The powerful baptism is the baptism with the Holy Spirit given by Jesus. The triune God is involved fully in this baptism as well: it was promised by the Father, bestowed by the Son, and performed by the Holy Spirit.

The baptism of the Holy Spirit is a vast and profound work in the life of the believer. Scores of books have been written trying to prove the veracity, the impact, and the importance or magnitude of this baptism. Yet all of these books would agree that an understanding of the baptism of the Holy Spirit is important to have. How do we accomplish that here without oversimplifying so that you, the reader, can move forward? The truth is, while the scope and impact of the Holy Spirit are full of divine mystery, the purpose is remarkably simple: this baptism—with the Holy Spirit and fire—is the coming of power and anointing upon an individual so that he may carry out his part of God's work.

Although the believer receives the Holy Spirit at conversion, the Spirit is released to work in the believer's life at the baptism with the Holy Spirit. Many would say that the positional baptism of 1 Corinthians 12:13 is the same as the powerful baptism of Luke 3:16. But if it is the same, then where is the power of God on your people? Where is the evidence in their character and witness? Where is the unmistakable seal of God's fire and power? You see, it just doesn't add up.

Most Christians have experienced positional and pictorial baptism but lack the baptism of power!

Sealed by the Spirit

One of the synonyms for the baptism of the Holy Spirit is the "seal of the Holy Spirit."

We're told in Ephesians 1:13 that "[in Christ] you were sealed with the Holy Spirit of promise." What is the seal, and how is it a description of the baptism of the Spirit? Clearly the Greek text indicates that this "sealing" came after conversion. All of the blessings of God flow into a believer's life when it has been taken over by the Spirit.

D. Martyn Lloyd-Jones, in his monumental six-volume commentary on Ephesians, declares that the Holy Spirit's sealing is God's mark of authenticity for every believer.[1] The Holy Spirit will "seal" or "mark" a believer by an outward action that gives authenticity to the believer. According to Lloyd-Jones, there are three main meanings to the word *seal* in the New Testament. They are "authenticity, authority, and ownership."[2]

The "seal" was not like our English word *seal*, which means to seal up like a jar or can. It means to mark by a brand or tag. When considering this seal, think about the logo on your favorite pair of jeans, sneakers, or purse. That mark gives an outward verification of the item's authenticity. Does a person need clarification when they see the distinctive swoosh that the product belongs to Nike? Consider the simple distinctiveness of the two overlapping "Cs"—the first inverted and the second forward facing—of the haute couture fashion house Chanel. Two handbags, identical in outward appearance, are discerned to be strikingly different when only one bears that famous seal. Consider also, that the "sealed" handbag is immediately considered to be of higher quality and greater value because of that mark. The baptism of the Holy Spirit with its subsequent outward manifestations is God's outward seal demonstrating His inner work on the life of a believer!

In John 20:22, the risen Christ breathes on the disciples, and they receive the Holy Spirit. Yet in Acts 1:4–5, He promises another work of the Spirit, the baptism with the Holy Spirit. Pentecost "sealed" with outward signs what had begun in the lives of the disciples. Looking at the situation logically, it appears that the disciples had everything they needed to go and fulfill the Great Commission that Jesus had given them. They had seen the risen Christ and communed with Him. Jesus breathed on them, and they received the Holy Spirit. Why then did Jesus tell them to go to Jerusalem and wait? I believe it is because the disciples needed more than a message and a heartfelt, sincere belief in a risen Christ. They needed God's *authority* to do the work He had called them to do.

Mentioned previously were the Samaritans in Acts 8:12. In that narrative, Philip believed that the Samaritans were saved, yet Acts 8:16 states, "As yet He [the Spirit] had fallen upon none of them." The baptism with the Holy Spirit is again seen as an outward sign! In Acts 9 Saul is converted but does not receive the baptism of the Holy Spirit until hands are laid upon him three days later. In Acts 19:2, at Ephesus, we find the same pattern: "Did you receive the Holy Spirit when you believed?" They had not heard of the Holy Spirit. Paul baptized them in water and then afterward laid hands on them, and they were baptized by the Spirit.

Thus the second work of the Holy Spirit is God's seal or mark that we are His. We belong to Him, and we are not ashamed of His power!

The Baptism or Seal Opens Heaven

In Ephesians 1:14, the work of the Spirit is described as "the guarantee" of our inheritance. The King James Version translates it as "the earnest" of our inheritance. The word has several meanings. The word was used for "down payment," a "promise," and an "engagement ring." The word is stronger than that in Greek. It means a portion of what is to come. Our "inheritance" is in the spiritual world. This is not difficult for anyone who has purchased a house to understand. When you search the market and find a house you like, you make an offer to buy. If that offer is accepted, *earnest money* must be paid. Once this money changes hands, this money is held in escrow until closing, and the seller cannot retract the offer. Once the earnest has been paid, the deal is essentially done.

Let's take just a moment to ponder the legal history of this practice and what we can learn from it. This money was known, in antiquity, as "God's penny," or *argentum Dei* (God's gold). Whenever money was exchanged for property, the money used to guarantee the sale, or the money used to show that the buyer and seller were both "earnest" about the transaction, was called God's gold. Our Father in heaven is so serious, so sincere, and so heartfelt in His longing to be with us and for us to be with Him that He is willing, and indeed joyfully able, to give us a small portion of the abundance that He has for us. He does so by giving us the baptism of the Holy Spirit, an "earnest payment," a small portion of the inheritance that is ours.

In 1 Peter 1:4 we're told that the fullness of this inheritance awaits us in heaven. In heaven there is health, not sickness; life, not death; abundance, not poverty; love, not hate; and joy, not sorrow! The baptism of the Holy Spirit moves to Earth now a portion of what is coming. This sealing or baptism with the Holy Spirit moves healing, blessings, gifts, fullness, love, life, joy, and hope to Earth now. The Holy Spirit's baptism brings the promise of God to Earth. This baptism is God's guarantee of everything He has promised us.

The Holy Spirit's baptism opens heaven and brings the resources of the spiritual world through you into your present circumstances. In 2 Corinthians 1:20–22 we see that an "anointing" comes to those who are "sealed," "marked," and baptized in the Holy Spirit.

> Oh, Holy Spirit, comfort me
> in times of grief and pain
> hold my heart within Thine own
> and bring joy to me again.
>
> At times I feel so all alone
> and I'm filled with such despair
> and all my hope and dreams are gone
> and that no one really cares.
>
> As I lift my eyes toward heaven
> and the tears begin to flow
> I cry, "Oh LORD, please help me
> I have nowhere else to go."
>
> And then I hear a gentle voice
> so soft but yet so clear
> this voice says, "I love you child
> and I am always here.
>
> "I will send My Holy Spirit
> to take away your sorrow
> to comfort you, my child,
> and help you face tomorrow."[3]

CHAPTER FIVE

The Baptism of the Holy Spirit in the New Testament

T HE KEY TO my whole new life was the baptism of the Holy Spirit. Others may choose another name for this experience, but I choose the biblical name. God came on me afresh and ushered me into His presence. I gained a more intimate walk with the Lord through this powerful release of God's presence on my life.

I believe that this climactic special moment is a mark on all of God's powerful servants of the past. Many speak of God's anointing as a sacred moment and the beginning of a new realm of ministry for them.

One of these mighty servants of history was R. A. Torrey. Torrey had been a Christian in the ministry for years when suddenly in the course of his Bible study, he found his attention strongly attracted to phrases in Scripture such as "filled with the Spirit," "the gift of the Holy Spirit," and "the Holy Spirit fell upon them." He wrote of his subsequent quest for the power of God in his own life:

> As I studied the subject still further, I became convinced that they described an experience which I did not myself possess, and I went to work to secure for myself the experience thus described. I sought earnestly that I might be "baptized with the Holy Spirit." I went

at it very ignorantly. I have often wondered if anyone ever went at it more ignorantly than I did. But while I was ignorant, I was thoroughly sincere and in earnest, and God met me, as He always meets the sincere and earnest soul, no matter how ignorant he may be. God gave me what I sought; I was baptized in the Holy Spirit. And the result was a transformed Christian life and a transformed ministry.[1]

Another man of God who refused to operate without the power of the Holy Spirit was D. L. Moody. Early in his ministry he pushed forward in his work, operating mostly in the strength of his own flesh. He felt he had no real power in his life, but he didn't know how to resolve that problem.

At the close of his meetings in a YMCA, two humble Free Methodist women often approached him and said, "We are praying for you." Their comment unnerved the young preacher. Finally one night on their approach, he asked, "Why are you praying for me? Why don't you pray for the unsaved?"

They responded, "We are praying that you may get the power." He asked what they meant, and they proceeded to explain to him the definite baptism of the Holy Spirit. He then prayed with the women, fervently desiring the power of God to fall on his life.

Not long after that prayer, as he was walking in the midst of the hustle and bustle of the streets of New York, the power of God fell upon Moody so mightily that he had to turn aside to the house of a friend. There, alone in a room for hours, he experienced a filling of his soul with such joy that he at last had to ask God to withhold His hand. He went out from there with the power of the Spirit upon him, and going directly to a London crusade, he saw God do a wondrous work through him, bringing hundreds into the church.[2]

I could write pages and pages of the men of God who have experienced the filling of the Spirit, such as Charles Spurgeon, Billy Sunday, Charles Finney, and Evan Roberts, the Welsh evangelist. However, God's power is not just for great preachers of the faith. It is God's desire for all Christians to know the power of the Holy Spirit upon them.

Look at Jesus

No one would deny that Jesus always had the Holy Spirit within Him. Yet at His baptism, all four Gospels agree: "He saw the Spirit of God descending...and alighting upon Him," and the Spirit "remained upon Him" (Matt. 3:16; John 1:32; see also Mark 3:10; Luke 3:11). Jesus received an equipping and anointing with power. If Jesus received such a blessing, who are we to deny the need in our own lives?

In Acts 10:37–38, Peter made reference to Jesus's anointing by the Holy Spirit in His sermon to the Gentile Cornelius's household:

> That word you know, which was proclaimed throughout all Judea, and began from Galilee after the baptism which John preached: how God anointed Jesus of Nazareth with the Holy Spirit and with power, who went about doing good and healing all who were oppressed by the devil, for God was with Him.

The result of this teaching on Cornelius and his company, as we're told in Acts 10:44, was the same experience: "The Holy Spirit fell upon all those who heard the word."

Many ask, "Couldn't someone get all of this at once?" The answer is yes. On rare occasions a person may be saved, empowered by the Spirit, and baptized in water on the same day. Most of us, however, have not had that kind of experience.

Some scholars believe that the sealing of the Holy Spirit in Ephesians 1:13 is the work of spiritual enduing subsequent to conversion. The great Anglican scholar D. Martyn Lloyd-Jones, A. J. Gordon, R. A. Torrey, and D. L. Moody are among those who believe in a special enduing of God's Holy Spirit.

The Apostles and the Holy Spirit

When you look at the apostles and their experience with the Holy Spirit, there is one clear pattern. The work of the Holy Spirit was a second work whereby a divine enabling came not simply within but upon them.

Let's review the evidence. Take Peter for example, who was in the upper room. In John 7:37–39 Peter heard the promise of the indwelling Holy Spirit. John 7:39 gives this disclaimer: "The Holy Spirit was not yet given, because Jesus was not yet glorified."

When Christ ascended on high in front of eyewitnesses, He entered the spiritual realm and took His seat at the right hand of God (Heb. 1:3). Jesus was exalted above all power and authorities, both visible and invisible (Eph. 1:20–21). All enemies were put under His feet (1 Cor. 15:25). Angels and demons were made subject to Him (1 Pet. 3:22).

Furthermore Jesus received authority at that moment to pour out the Holy Spirit on the church. On the Day of Pentecost, Peter said, "Having received from the Father the promise of the Holy Spirit, He poured out this which you now see and hear" (Acts 2:33).

Peter was experiencing and sharing what both the Old Testament and Jesus had promised! In Peter's and the disciples' experience they heard the promise and even received the indwelling Spirit prior to Pentecost.

In John 20:22, before Pentecost, Jesus "breathed on them, and said to them, 'Receive the Holy Spirit.'" For Peter and the other disciples, what happened *in* them came *upon* them on the Day of Pentecost. In Acts 1:5 we read the promise and instruction: "For John truly baptized with water, but you shall be baptized with the Holy Spirit not many days from now."

The words *shall be baptized with the Holy Spirit* are in the future passive indicative. This means that what was coming to the upper room had not happened before. It is passive indicative that this was God's work upon a person! Obviously the disciples were saved and had received the Holy Spirit prior to this divine moment.

Baptism With the Spirit Described

Acts 1:8 describes and defines the baptism with the Holy Spirit: "You shall receive power when the Holy Spirit has come upon you; and you shall be witnesses to Me in Jerusalem, and in all Judea and Samaria, and to the end of the earth."

Notice the Holy Spirit comes "upon" the believer, *then* power comes. This is an outward demonstration of power. This power releases a witness that can change the whole earth. So many pastors want to teach that believers can live power-filled lives, but they do so while teaching that the believer does not need the baptism of the Holy Spirit!

It is important to notice the Greek expression "upon." It comes from two words: *ep*, which means "upon," and *erchomas*, which means "to *come* suddenly." The word can be translated "to attack."

Clearly then the disciples were told to expect outward manifestations upon the arrival of the baptism with the Spirit.

That is exactly what happened when you read the record

in Acts 2:1–4. A powerful transformation occurred in the disciples as fear left and power came! Later in Acts you find the same pattern with Paul. Three days after his conversion, he is baptized with the Spirit. As we have indicated earlier, the same pattern is repeated throughout the Book of Acts (Acts 8:12–17; 19).

Clearly the baptism with the Holy Spirit was God's endowment to complete the work of the church in the earth. Furthermore, this experience blurred the lines between the spiritual realm and the earthly realm. The power of the heavenly realm breaks into our world through those who welcome the Holy Spirit.

What the Baptism With the Holy Spirit Is Not

The baptism with the Holy Spirit is the forerunner of all the graces and gifts of the Spirit. Let me make it clear what the baptism with the Spirit is not.

First, and most importantly, the baptism with the Holy Spirit is not salvation or conversion, as we have already written. It comes after one has believed.

Second, the baptism with the Holy Spirit is not to be confused with water baptism. This act is only a picture of God placing the believer into Christ.

Third, the baptism with the Holy Spirit is not the gifts of the Spirit. Many believe that the only evidence of Spirit baptism is the gift of tongues or a prayer language. These teachers, good-intentioned though I am certain they are, even go so far as to say that tongues is the singular initial evidence of the Holy Spirit baptism, and if a believer has not spoken in tongues, then that believer has not received the baptism of the Holy Spirit. While I believe that tongues is *one* evidence, and probably the most prolific evidence, there is no clear Scripture reference or proof in early church history that this was the definitive sign. There are at least nineteen gifts of the Spirit, and *all* are important. Please understand that I believe *every* Christian can have a prayer language and that tongues are important and necessary in the life of believers and the church. Furthermore, tongues are a sign of apostolic flow and power that all may enjoy. Let us not say more than Scripture says. The baptism with the Holy Spirit releases the gifts. These gifts include, but are not limited to or necessarily prefaced by, speaking in tongues.

Fourth, the baptism with the Spirit is not the fruit of the Spirit. These attitudes are released by the indwelling Spirit and flow from the heart of the growing believer. Love, joy, peace, and the other attitudes released by the Spirit are important and follow the baptism with the Spirit.

Fifth, the baptism with the Holy Spirit is not the filling of the Holy Spirit. As I have written, the baptism with the Holy Spirit is a decisive event after one believes that makes fullness possible!

In Ephesians 5:18 we read, "Be not drunk with wine, wherein is excess; but be filled with the Spirit" (KJV). In the original language, this passage is in the present active imperative. That means it is a continuous, commanded experience. The "baptism or sealing" with the Spirit is a defining moment whereby the believer is forever marked by the eternal Word *living in us*!

CHAPTER SIX
The Baptism of the Holy Spirit as Your Inheritance

C LEARLY CONNECTED TO the baptism with the Holy Spirit is the word *inheritance*. Ephesians 1:13–14 speaks of believers being "sealed" by the Spirit and that this sealing, or as we have seen, this baptism, is a down payment or guarantee of our inheritance.

Long ago Job asked a question that still resonates with every believer today: "What is the allotment of God from above, and the inheritance of the Almighty from on high?" (Job 31:2). Even the disciples would come to Jesus listing all they had given up and asking about what they would have in the kingdom. In Mark 10:28–30, the disciples protested to Jesus that they had "left all" to go with Him. Jesus promised them a "hundred-fold" in this life! I believe the baptism with the Holy Spirit is the key to tapping into your inheritance now!

In contemporary terms, the question will be, "What's in it for me?" On the surface that sounds callous, but God gives us our desires and enjoys blessing us. Listen to this promise in Psalm 37:4: "Delight yourself also in the LORD, and He shall give you the desires of your heart."

God is not a stingy, penny-pinching Lord but a generous, joyful Father! He wants us to know the abundant life. Jesus details the differences between Himself and Satan (and by

34

extension, I would think, those who follow each respectively) in John 10:10 when He says:

> The thief does not come except to steal, and to kill, and to destroy. I have come that they may have life, and that they may have it more abundantly.

You Are an Heir!

One thing you must know is that a benefit of coming to Christ is you become part of a family! Ephesians 2:15 tells us that Jesus, "having abolished in His flesh the enmity, that is, the law of commandments contained in ordinances, so as to create in Himself one new man from the two, thus making peace," causes us to be "no longer strangers and foreigners, but fellow citizens with the saints and members of the household of God" (v. 19). Because of Jesus, you are a part of a new race of men and a new family. So what do you need to know about this family?

1. You were born into it! John 3:3 says, "Jesus answered and said to him, 'Most assuredly, I say to you, unless one is born again, he cannot see the kingdom of God.'"

2. You were delivered from the old tyrannical domain of Satan and transferred to a new realm. Colossians 1:13 states, "He has delivered us from the power of darkness and conveyed us into the kingdom of the Son of His love."

3. You are now an heir of God. Romans 8:16–17 says, "The Spirit Himself bears witness with our spirit that we are children of God, and if children, then heirs—heirs of God and joint heirs

with Christ, if indeed we suffer with Him, that
we may also be glorified together."

Your Covenant Inheritance

Jesus Christ redeemed us from the curse by His death, paid
our debt, and has called us to an eternal inheritance. We read
in Hebrews 9:15, "And for this reason He is the Mediator of
the new covenant, by means of death, for the redemption of
the transgressions under the first covenant, that those who are
called may receive the promise of the eternal inheritance."

As heirs of God, you now have access to the benefits of an
inheritance that can never be exhausted! It is forever unlim-
ited. Everything in the natural on Earth will end at death.
Your benefits in the inheritance roll into your eternal domain
with you!

1. You have access to God's wisdom. Ecclesiastes
   7:11 says, "Wisdom is good with an inheritance, and profitable to those who see the sun."
   Wisdom is necessary for those who would
   wisely use their inheritance!

2. God becomes your portion. Your inheritance is
   God Himself! Psalm 16:5 reads, "O LORD, You
   are the portion of my inheritance and my cup;
   You maintain my lot."

The New Testament gives the same promise of revelation
knowledge! You have inside access to God's wisdom. Wisdom,
in Scripture, is knowing what to do!

Notice that this inheritance comes with the Holy Spirit
(more on this later). It is guaranteed, and it releases revelation knowledge and the spirit of wisdom. This opens your

spiritual eyes to see all that God has for you. Look closely at God's management of your life. There are seven gifts of God's wisdom and five promises of your inheritance in Him.

The Seven Gifts of God's Wisdom

1. God orders your steps: "The steps of a good man are ordered by the LORD, and He delights in his way" (Ps. 37:23).

2. God gives good things: "The lines have fallen to me in pleasant places; yes, I have a good inheritance" (Ps. 16:6).

3. God gives counsel through dreams and visions: "I will bless the LORD who has given me counsel; my heart also instructs me in the night seasons" (Ps. 16:7).

4. An awareness of His continual presence: "I have set the LORD always before me; because He is at my right hand I shall not be moved" (Ps. 16:8).

5. Removal of fleshly anxiety: "Therefore my heart is glad, and my glory rejoices; my flesh also will rest in hope" (Ps. 16:9).

6. Clear direction for the abundant life: "For You will not leave my soul in Sheol, nor will You allow Your Holy One to see corruption. You will show me the path of life" (Ps. 16:10–11). God will bring us out of that which kills, separates, and destroys.

7. Fills us with joy and pleasure: "In Your presence is fullness of joy; at Your right hand are pleasures forevermore" (Ps. 16:11).

Five Promises of Your Inheritance

In Psalm 37, David instructs us on the fivefold benefit of our inheritance.

1. A lifetime guarantee: "The LORD knows the days of the upright, and their inheritance shall be forever" (Ps. 37:18). All of our earthly stuff has a time and wear limit! God gives us a lasting release of favor.

2. Life of fullness at all times: "They shall not be ashamed in the evil time, and in the days of famine they shall be satisfied" (Ps. 37:19). Even when things are bad and evil lifts its ugly head, God will satisfy!

3. A generous prosperity: "But the wicked shall perish; and the enemies of the LORD, like the splendor of the meadows, shall vanish. Into smoke they shall vanish away. The wicked borrows and does not repay, but the righteous shows mercy and gives. For those blessed by Him shall inherit the earth, but those cursed by Him shall be cut off" (Ps. 37:20–22). Here it is clear that those who are heirs of God understand the power of giving and will receive financial prosperity.

4. Recovery from failure: "The steps of a good man are ordered by the LORD, and He delights in his way. Though he fall, he shall not be utterly cast down; for the LORD upholds him with His hand" (Ps. 37:23–24). Here again we see the benefit of God's direction. Along the way we may

fall, but God is holding our hand. He allows us to learn from those times we leave His path. He still holds our hand and lifts us up! Hallelujah! If you let go, He holds on; no man can pluck you out of His hand!

5. A lasting legacy: "I have been young, and now am old; yet I have not seen the righteous forsaken, nor his descendants begging bread" (Ps. 37:25). Here is the promise that you can pass down what God has given. He will not forsake us or those who follow us!

Activating Your Inheritance

Now that you are beginning to see some aspects of your inheritance, you might ask, "What is the protocol necessary for receiving my inheritance?" Above all else, you must be positioned to receive and enjoy these benefits and promises.

1. You must be in the kingdom. You enter the kingdom by the new birth, by being saved! Acts 26:17–18 states, "I will deliver you from the Jewish people, as well as from the Gentiles, to whom I now send you, to open their eyes, in order to turn them from darkness to light, and from the power of Satan to God, that they may receive forgiveness of sins and an inheritance among those who are sanctified by faith in Me." Salvation opens your spiritual eyes and reveals your sin. Additionally, salvation delivers you from Satan's power, forgives your sin, and offers the full potential of your inheritance.

2. You must love the church: Acts 26:18 talks about "an inheritance among those who are sanctified by faith." This promise is for those who know they are "among" a gathering of other heirs!

3. You must receive the sealing, the baptism of the Holy Spirit. As a part of the family even without the baptism of the Holy Spirit, you dwell in "the rain" you receive from the overflow of what is going on in those who are filled. Yet the greatest release comes to those who are "sealed," or marked by the Holy Spirit. As we're told in Ephesians 1:12–14, "That we who first trusted in Christ should be to the praise of His glory. In Him you also trusted, after you heard the word of truth, the gospel of your salvation; in whom also, having believed, you were sealed with the Holy Spirit of promise, who is the guarantee of our inheritance until the redemption of the purchased possession, to the praise of His glory." Until the rapture of the church, the sealing of the Holy Spirit is the guarantor of every benefit and promise of our inheritance. This sealing is often an outward sign in the life of a believer.

4. You must have faith in the supernatural realm of God.

The inheritance that is yours now can only be activated by faith! Look at these two verses:

> So now, brethren, I commend you to God and to the
> word of His grace, which is able to build you up and give
> you an inheritance among all those who are sanctified.
>
> —ACTS 20:32

> To open their eyes, in order to turn them from dark-
> ness to light, and from the power of Satan to God, that
> they may receive forgiveness of sins and an inheritance
> among those who are sanctified by faith in Me.
>
> —ACTS 26:18

The Word promises the gifts of an inheritance. Faith sanc-
tifies or sets you apart from the rest to claim your inheritance.

In *Rain Man*, the classic movie about autism, Charlie Babbitt, played by Tom Cruise, receives notice of his father's death.
He returns home to discover that millions of dollars have been
left to his autistic brother, Raymond or "Rain Man."[1] Think
about this: Charlie Babbitt missed his inheritance because he
abandoned his father, disregarded his word, never understood
his heart, and did not believe in what he had done. So many
today are missing their inheritance because they do not like
how God the Father chooses to operate. Here are some things
you need to know:

1. Prayer releases the inheritance. You must stay in
   touch to receive what God has. Psalm 2:8 says,
   "Ask of Me, and I will give You the nations for
   Your inheritance, and the ends of the earth for
   Your possession." God says, "Ask Me" and the
   world is yours! Prayer moves the resources of the
   earth and heaven into place for believers.

2. Angels bring assistance to heirs. Controver-
   sial? Maybe. Does this mean we pray to or worship angels? Absolutely not! But look at what

Hebrews 1:14 has to say about angels: "Are they not all ministering spirits sent forth to minister for those who will inherit salvation?" Heavenly hosts, warring angels, reaping angels, and strengthening angels are all around. They operate for those who are heirs!

3. Miraculous wealth transfers from the world funds the inheritance. God can bless us with money from the enemy's coffers! Solomon states it as a fact in Proverbs 13:22 when he says, "A good man leaves an inheritance to his children's children, but the wealth of the sinner is stored up for the righteous." Remember also the wonderful promise from Jesus in the Beatitudes when He said, "Blessed are the meek, for they shall inherit the earth" (Matt. 5:5).

Some Cautions About Your Inheritance

It's easy to hear all of these things and get excited, but we must remember that, just as in every covenant relationship, there are two sides to the equation: promises *and* conditions. We've seen some of the promises, so what are the conditions?

Act like an heir in every circumstance

Some (possibly many or even all) of the members of the church at Colosse were employed, for lack of a better word, as hostlers (think person who cleans up the stuff you don't want to) in Caesar's stables. What a thankless job! Yet the apostle Paul encouraged them by saying, "Obey in all things your masters according to the flesh, not with eyeservice, as men-pleasers, but in sincerity of heart, fearing God. And whatever you do, do it heartily, as to the Lord and not to men, knowing that from the Lord you will receive the reward of the inheritance; for you serve the Lord Christ. But he who does wrong will be repaid for what he has done, and there is no partiality" (Col. 3:22–25). The Colossians may have been mucking out stables, but they knew a better life was coming for them—and it did!

Live a transformed lifestyle

This goes beyond "but be transformed by the renewing of your mind" (though that portion is vital). Paul reminded the Galatians that "the works of the flesh are evident, which are: adultery, fornication, uncleanness, lewdness, idolatry, sorcery, hatred, contentions, jealousies, outbursts of wrath, selfish ambitions, dissensions, heresies, envy, murders, drunkenness, revelries, and the like; of which I tell you beforehand, just as I also told you in time past, that those who practice such things will not inherit the kingdom of God. But the fruit of the Spirit is love, joy, peace, longsuffering, kindness, goodness, faithfulness, gentleness, self-control. Against such there is no law. And those who are Christ's have crucified the flesh with its passions and desires. If we live in the Spirit, let us also walk in the Spirit" (Gal. 5:19–25).

Remember also that no matter how social values and mores may change, the Bible is clear that "no fornicator, unclean person, nor covetous man, who is an idolater, has any inheritance in the kingdom of Christ and God" (Eph. 5:5). This verse makes it clear that immorality does not steal your salvation but limits your blessings. This list is expanded in 1 Corinthians 6:9–10, where it states, "Do you not know that the unrighteous will not inherit the kingdom of God? Do not be deceived. Neither fornicators, nor idolaters, nor adulterers, nor homosexuals, nor sodomites, nor thieves, nor covetous, nor drunkards, nor revilers, nor extortioners will inherit the kingdom of God." But then the glorious reminder: "*And such were some of you. But you were washed, but you were sanctified, but you were justified in the name of the Lord Jesus and by the Spirit of our God*" (v. 11, emphasis added). In the simplest of terms, we are called out of ungodly lifestyles.

We don't have to do this in our own power. We should remember, like Isaiah, that "because the Sovereign LORD helps me, I will not be disgraced. Therefore have I set my face like flint, and I know I will not be put to shame" (Isa. 50:7, NIV).

Live an overcoming life

This might sound like a conditional command, but it is, more than anything else, a wonderful promise that God will enable us to be, as it says in Romans 8:37, "more than conquerors through Him who loved us." Listen to these promises:

> Let God be true but every man a liar. As it is written: "That You may be justified in Your words, and may overcome when You are judged."
>
> —ROMANS 3:4

> Do not be overcome by evil, but overcome evil with good.
>
> —ROMANS 12:21

> [Give] thanks to the Father who has qualified us to be partakers of the inheritance of the saints in the light. *He has delivered us from the power of darkness* and conveyed us into the kingdom of the Son of His love.
>
> —COLOSSIANS 1:12–13, EMPHASIS ADDED

Support Israel

This need not be a political issue. God's view on this situation was made clear when He promised Abram, "I will bless those who bless you, and I will curse him who curses you" (Gen. 12:3). It really is that simple.

Never let wealth diminish your relationship with God

There is probably no sadder story of an interaction with Jesus than that of the rich young ruler found in Luke 18:18–23. Before any discussion, read this story again.

> Now a certain ruler asked Him, saying, "Good Teacher, what shall I do to inherit eternal life?" So Jesus said to him, "Why do you call Me good? No one is good but One, that is, God. You know the commandments: 'Do not commit adultery,' 'Do not murder,' 'Do not steal,' 'Do not bear false witness,' 'Honor your father and your mother.'" And he said, "All these things I have kept from my youth." So when Jesus heard these things, He said to him, "You still lack one thing. Sell all that you have and distribute to the poor, and you will have treasure in heaven; and come, follow Me." But when he heard this, he became very sorrowful, for he was very rich.

Before saying anything else about this young man, let's observe the facts. He was obviously sincere in his desire to be obedient to God. He sought out Jesus and acknowledged Him as "good." He had kept all of the commandments "from his youth." But look at Jesus's first interaction with him: "Why do you call Me good? No one is good but One, that is, God."

Why did Jesus do this? It seems very confrontational and questions the young man's intentions from the outset. But Jesus knew something that we didn't. This rich young ruler valued his money more than God. That's why Jesus asked the question He did, and it's also why Jesus told him to sell all he, the young man, had: because Jesus knew that to this rich young ruler, money was god!

Control your attitude toward others

In this "dog-eat-dog" world, there is a prevalent attitude of entitlement and greed. Justice is measured in the swiftness and severity of retribution. But 1 Peter 3:9–12 tells us we are to be a compassionate people, "not returning evil for evil or reviling for reviling, but on the contrary blessing, knowing that you were called to this, that you may inherit a blessing. For 'He who would love life and see good days, let him refrain his tongue from evil, and his lips from speaking deceit. Let him turn away from evil and do good; let him seek peace and pursue it. For the eyes of the LORD are on the righteous, and His ears are open to their prayers; but the face of the LORD is against those who do evil.'" Revenge, getting even, arguing, gossiping, criticizing, running your mouth, and lying forfeit kingdom blessing.

Instead we are to be:

- ◆ In unity
- ◆ Compassionate
- ◆ Serving in love
- ◆ Doing good
- ◆ Seeking and pursuing peace

If we do these, we "inherit a blessing" and "love life and see good days."

CHAPTER SEVEN
God's Endowment for Ministry

THE BAPTISM OF the Holy Spirit releases supernatural enabling for practical service. In the Old Testament promise, the New Testament fulfillment, and throughout church history the baptism with the Spirit empowered the church to impact the culture.

Larry Hart, professor of theology at Oral Roberts University (and a PhD graduate of Southern Baptist Theological Seminary in Louisville, Kentucky), has given an excellent survey of this truth.[1] He points out that in the Old Testament, the Spirit came upon individuals to perform heroic deeds for God's people.[2] Also, the Spirit enabled practical works to be done, such as when Bezalel was given gifts to design and build the tabernacle (Exod. 31). Joseph was given wisdom by the Spirit (Gen. 41:38). In the New Testament, the Spirit came on Pentecost to abide upon each member of the church to release witness and service on them (Acts 1:8).[3]

Testimony of History

Across every segment of church history we find the affirmation of the same truths. Both Tertullian and Hilary of Poitiers believed that the pattern of Jesus's water baptism, which was followed by the Spirit descending upon Him, should be the model for all members of the church.[4] Tertullian, who preached to more than five thousand each Sunday in the third century, affirmed the charismatic gifts.[5]

Hilary of Poitiers was also an early church father and leader who was exiled for his spiritual fervor.[6] His book on Christian initiation declares that the *charisma* (or gifts) were released as a part of the regular works experienced by the church in her first eight centuries. "God has instituted them," said Hilary.[7] He also insisted that they are not "adornments" but are to be used for witness and ministry.[8]

In describing the baptism of the Holy Spirit, Hilary said, "The Holy Spirit is called a river. When we receive the Holy Spirit, we are made drunk. Because out of us as a source, various streams of grace flow, the prophet prays that the Lord will inebriate us. The prophet wants the same people made drunk and filled to all fullness with the divine gifts, so that their generation may be multiplied."[9]

Your Promise for Today

As you can see, what the baptism of the Spirit releases today is consistent with Scripture and early church history. There can be no denial of Spirit baptism and the subsequent release of spiritual gifts. What then can we expect when the baptism with the Holy Spirit occurs?

First, the Holy Spirit restores an intimate relationship with God as Father. In Galatians 4:6, the outpoured Spirit cries "Abba, Father" as He comes upon the believer. The believer, upon realizing this wonderful truth, cries back, "Abba, Father." Abba is the affectionate word for "daddy" or "papa" in the ancient language. Could it be that a clear evidence of Spirit baptism is a powerful revelation that individual believers have come home? How important it is for the church to communicate this healing truth to all Spirit-baptized believers.

Second, the Holy Spirit's power was given for the purpose of witness and missions. Remember that Jesus said in Acts 1:8 that the disciples would "receive power when the Holy Spirit has come upon you; and you shall be witnesses to Me in Jerusalem, and in all Judea and Samaria, and to the end of the earth."

Included in this mandate would be the liberation of the believer from Satan's dominion to a new level of freedom, from the demonic spirit of fear into one "of power and of love and of a sound mind" (2 Tim. 2:7). Further, remember that our victory is certain because "they overcame him by the blood of the Lamb and by the word of their testimony, and they did not love their lives to the death" (Rev. 12:11).

As a part of this commission, the baptism of the Holy Spirit would be accompanied by spiritual gifts, signs, and wonders to confirm the witness. Look at the details of Mark 16:15–20:

> And He said to them, "Go into all the world and preach the gospel to every creature. He who believes and is baptized will be saved; but he who does not believe will be condemned. And these signs will follow those who believe: In My name they will cast out demons; they will speak with new tongues; they will take up serpents; and if they drink anything deadly, it will by no means hurt them; they will lay hands on the sick, and they will recover." So then, after the Lord had spoken to them, He was received up into heaven, and sat down at the right hand of God. And they went out and preached everywhere, the Lord working with them and confirming the word through the accompanying signs. Amen.

The church's worldwide mission was to be confirmed with signs and wonders. Clear evidence of Spirit-baptized witness was casting out demons, speaking in tongues, divine protection, and healing miracles.

Third, the Holy Spirit's baptism would result in mental and emotional transformation. Instead of old attitudes of hatred, impatience, pride, revenge, and indulgence, the Holy Spirit would release "love, joy, peace, longsuffering, gentleness, goodness, faith, meekness, temperance" (Gal. 5:22–23, KJV). Here radical transformation of human character became possible. The baptism of the Spirit enables a new culture of love for humanity.

It is important to understand that agape love, a love that serves others, is the hallmark of true Christianity. Jesus declared that love would be the key mark of generating faith. Paul makes it clear in Romans 5:1–5 that this love is not an emotion but a work of the Holy Spirit.

> Therefore, having been justified by faith, we have peace with God through our Lord Jesus Christ, through whom also we have access by faith into this grace in which we stand, and rejoice in hope of the glory of God. And not only that, but we also glory in tribulations, knowing that tribulation produces perseverance; and perseverance, character; and character, hope. Now hope does not disappoint, because the love of God has been poured out in our hearts by the Holy Spirit who was given to us.

This powerful outpouring of love keeps the believer strong through seasons of suffering and difficulty.

Fourth, the baptism with the Holy Spirit brings special enlightenment, wisdom, and understanding to the believer. For today's Christian, it is important to understand and be established in "present truth" (2 Pet. 1:12). God's Word has present application, predictions, and insights. The Holy Spirit releases the "mind of Christ," the very thoughts of God. Through a believer's spirit, the Holy Spirit opens the eyes of one's inner man (Eph. 1:17–18).

The hope that believers would embrace such a wonderful offer drove Paul to his knees. Look here at the great apostolic prayer that sets forth the powerful potential of great accomplishment by the church.

> [I pray] that [God] would grant you, according to the riches of His glory, to be strengthened with might through His Spirit in the inner man, that Christ may dwell in your hearts through faith; that you, being rooted and grounded in love, may be able to comprehend with all the saints what is the width and length and depth and height—to know the love of Christ which passes knowledge; that you may be filled with all the fullness of God. Now to Him who is able to do exceedingly abundantly above all that we ask or think, according to the power that works in us, to Him be glory in the church by Christ Jesus to all generations, forever and ever. Amen.
>
> —EPHESIANS 3:16–21

Here we see spiritual strength, comprehension, supernatural knowledge, fullness, and ability released to the church.

It is critically important to understand that the graces and gifts released by the baptism of the Spirit are without limit. We could recite the possibilities without end. Yet there are clear parameters. The church should be the setting for the charismatic gifts to operate, not some split parachurch group or some cult setting. The church must welcome the Holy Spirit. Those who have used the baptism of the Spirit to divide must come home to the church. The church can reach her potential if we unify around the work of the Spirit.

CHAPTER EIGHT
Physical Manifestations of the Baptism of the Holy Spirit

A FALL OF GOD'S power will bring encouragement. The Bible describes these times as "times of refreshing" (Acts 3:19). God sends a refreshing shower of spiritual life on the dry desert of our hearts. When we are burned out and want to quit, the blessed Holy Spirit shows up. Spiritual thirst brings on the refreshing shower of blessing. God promises, "For I will pour water on him who is thirsty, and floods on the dry ground; I will pour My Spirit on your descendants, and My blessing on your offspring" (Isa. 44:3).

When God's power falls, there will also be endowment. God pours out His gifts upon the church to equip it for ministry. Times of revival bring forth a fresh release of spiritual abilities to the church. Revival is a showcase of what man can do as God breaks through in His power.

In addition, when God shows up, there will be a special enduing on a person. Jesus promised, "Behold, I send the Promise of My Father upon you; but tarry in the city of Jerusalem until you are endued with power from on high" (Luke 24:49).

The word *endue* actually means "to clothe." This has to do with the visible work of the Holy Spirit. Just as you can see clothing on an individual's body, this enduing is the tangible evidence that God has come upon a person's spirit.

How does the Holy Spirit manifest Himself? In other chapters we studied some of the gifts, such as tongues, and other phenomena. Let's now look at a few other manifestations whereby the Spirit shows Himself.

Shaking or Trembling

Trembling has been a regular occurrence in many services of our church. Trembling can be mild or convulsive. God's Word includes numerous incidents where people trembled under God's power. Often the trembling was a result of fear in His presence.

> "Do you not fear Me?" says the LORD.
> "Will you not tremble at My presence,
> Who have placed the sand as the bound of the sea,
> By a perpetual decree, that it cannot pass beyond it?
> And though its waves toss to and fro,
> Yet they cannot prevail;
> Though they roar, yet they cannot pass over it."
>
> —JEREMIAH 5:22

> And he said to me, "O Daniel, man greatly beloved, understand the words that I speak to you, and stand upright, for I have now been sent to you." While he was speaking this word to me, I stood trembling. Then he said to me, "Do not fear, Daniel, for from the first day that you set your heart to understand, and to humble yourself before your God, your words were heard; and I have come because of your words."
>
> —DANIEL 10:11–12

When I heard, my body trembled;
My lips quivered at the voice;
Rottenness entered my bones;
And I trembled in myself,
That I might rest in the day of trouble.

—HABAKKUK 3:16

Other times, trembling occurred when someone was delivered or healed. In Mark 5:33 we find that the woman healed of the issue of blood trembled under the reality of what she had been delivered from: "But the woman, fearing and trembling, knowing what had happened to her, came and fell down before Him and told Him the whole truth."

In addition, individuals were known to tremble under the convicting power of the Holy Spirit, as recorded in Acts 24:25: "And as he reasoned of righteousness, temperance, and judgment to come Felix trembled, and answered, Go thy way for this time; when I have a convenient season, I will call for thee" (KJV). Acts 9:6 records Paul's conversion when he, "trembling and astonished," asked God for new direction.

Every incident of the Spirit's filling in the New Testament does not indicate trembling, but it certainly is possible. In Acts 4:31 the entire room was shaken as the apostles received the baptism of the Holy Spirit.

Trembling was common during the Great Awakening and is certainly a legitimate expression of the conviction of the Holy Spirit. This manifestation gave the early American Quakers their name. Reverend Barton Stone, a leader of the Cane Ridge revival, told in his 1847 autobiography of the many bodily "exercises" he witnessed at frontier revivals:

Sometimes the subject of the jerks would be affected in some one member of the body, and sometimes in the whole system. When the head alone was affected, it would be jerked backward and forward, or from side to side, so quickly that the features of the face could not be distinguished. When the whole system was affected, I have seen the person stand in one place, and jerk backward and forward in quick succession, their head nearly touching the floor behind and before.[1]

A young man once wrote out his testimony concerning his experiences of this nature.

During a Sunday morning service, God prompted me to raise my hands during a particular worship chorus. Normally I wouldn't argue with Him, but I didn't really like the song this time! His Spirit kept insisting, and so I obeyed. When I did, my hands began to shake. It was a wonderful feeling! After a couple of other choruses, the shaking stopped. As I reflected on the experience, I recalled that early in the service, I had asked God to touch me in a special way. These "kisses from the Father" have a way of releasing me from any pride and taking me out of my comfort zone. He has a way of coming out of that little box I try to put Him in and showing Himself to be more awesome than I ever imagined.

Joy and Singing

Every so often a holy laughter and an outbreak of joy accompany a movement of the Holy Spirit. Two scriptures immediately come to mind when I think of the joy surrounding the Word of God:

Then was our mouth filled with laughter, and our tongue with singing: then said they among the heathen, The LORD hath done great things for them.

—PSALM 126:2, KJV

> A time to weep, and a time to laugh; a time to mourn,
> and a time to dance.
> —ECCLESIASTES 3:4

Although these verses don't instruct us specifically in the use of laughter by the Holy Spirit, you can't get away from the fact that freedom from the bondage of the enemy produces real joy. Salvation is a *rescue*! What happened to the Israelites in the natural often is applicable to the spiritual realm. First Corinthians 10:11 indicates that they are "examples" to us. The joy resulting from freedom may lead to a continuing desire to sing and to praise Jesus. Simon Peter knew this truth when he wrote:

> In this you greatly rejoice, though now for a little while, if need be, you have been grieved by various trials, that the genuineness of your faith, being much more precious than gold that perishes, though it is tested by fire, may be found to praise, honor, and glory at the revelation of Jesus Christ, whom having not seen you love. Though now you do not see Him, yet believing, you rejoice with joy inexpressible and full of glory.
> —1 PETER 1:6–8

Jonathan Edwards, in his book *Religious Affections*, told of many instances during his meetings when people would burst into laughter and moments later be melted into tears when the Spirit fell.[2]

In many revivals, this joy would express itself in singing. An example comes from the testimony of George Whitefield:

> Soon after this I found and felt in myself that I was delivered from the burden that had so heavily oppressed me; the spirit of mourning was taken from me and I knew what it was truly to rejoice in God my Saviour, and for some time could not avoid singing psalms

wherever I was. But my joy gradually became more set-
tled and, blessed be God, has abode and increased in my
soul, saving a few casual intermissions, ever since. Thus
were the days of my mourning ended.[3]

Again, we read Reverend Stone's account of the beautiful
singing of people touched by the Spirit in his day:

This singing exercise is more unaccountable than anything else I ever saw. The subject in a very happy state of
mind would sing most melodiously, not from the mouth
or nose, but entirely in the breast, the sounds issuing
thence. Such music silenced everything, and attracted
the attention of all. It was most heavenly. None could
ever be tired of hearing it.[4]

Drunkenness or Euphoria

On the Day of Pentecost, an accusation leveled against the
apostles was drunkenness. Look at these verses once more:

Others mocking said, "They are full of new wine." But
Peter, standing up with the eleven, raised his voice and
said to them, "Men of Judea and all who dwell in Jerusalem, let this be known to you, and heed my words.
For these are not drunk, as you suppose, since it is only
the third hour of the day."

—ACTS 2:13–15

Notice also the words of Jeremiah:

My heart within me is broken because of the prophets;
all my bones shake. I am like a drunken man, and like
a man whom wine has overcome, because of the LORD,
and because of His holy words.

—JEREMIAH 23:9

Paul later taught that it was possible to be drunk on the Holy Spirit. Just as some men fill up their bellies with wine and are influenced by its power, so can the believer become powered by the fullness of the Spirit.

> Do not be drunk with wine, in which is dissipation; but be filled with the Spirit, speaking to one another in psalms and hymns and spiritual songs, singing and making melody in your heart to the Lord, giving thanks always for all things to God the Father in the name of our Lord Jesus Christ, submitting to one another in the fear of God.
>
> —EPHESIANS 5:18–21

This verse is not a contrast but a comparison. Being filled with the Spirit may cause you to do some things you may not usually do. Some people experience a sense of dizziness or euphoria when they experience this filling. While these manifestations may occur, more importantly, the Holy Spirit will create in you a fresh hunger for Scripture, a new love for Jesus, and a new display of the fruit of the Spirit in your life.

Crying and Weeping

Hardly anyone would question the validity of tears as a spiritual reflection of God's move. God cherishes the tears of His people. David recorded his prayer:

> You number my wanderings;
> Put my tears into Your bottle;
> Are they not in Your book?
>
> —PSALM 56:8

One may also seek the Lord with tears:

> My tears have been my food day and night,
> While they continually say to me,
> "Where is your God?"
>
> —PSALM 42:3

Repentance and concern bring tears. When revival broke out under Nehemiah, there was much loud weeping.

> And Nehemiah, who was the governor, Ezra the priest and scribe, and the Levites who taught the people said to all the people, "This day is holy to the LORD your God; do not mourn nor weep." For all the people wept, when they heard the words of the Law.
>
> —NEHEMIAH 8:9

It is comforting to know that God is responsive to our weeping, as we see in 2 Chronicles 34:27:

> "Because your heart was tender, and you humbled yourself before God when you heard His words against this place and against its inhabitants, and you humbled yourself before Me, and you tore your clothes and wept before Me, I also have heard you," says the LORD.

Jeremiah wept over the spiritual condition of Israel:

> Oh, that my head were waters, and my eyes a fountain of tears, that I might weep day and night for the slain of the daughter of my people!
>
> —JEREMIAH 9:1

Jesus Christ wept publicly and unashamedly; on one occasion a woman who had been of questionable reputation wept over His feet and dried them with her hair (Luke 7:38). The apostle Paul wept with the Ephesian elders as he left their city.

He reminded them of his ministry of tears during the time that he served with them.

Perhaps the most telling scriptural example of tears in the church is the parable of the sinner's prayer found in Luke 18. Remember that the synagogue was the forerunner of the early church, and it was a place of expression. A Pharisee and a tax collector went into the synagogue to pray. The Pharisee spoke forth a glittering prayer that was filled with pride, but the tax collector beat upon his breast and cried, "God, be merciful to me a sinner!" (Luke 18:13). Jesus commented that the tax collector was justified because of his humility.

We need more of that kind of humility in our churches today. Loud weeping may often be a part of true revival. We are seeing it today when God breaks through.

Dancing and Bodily Movements

The word *praise* is often tied to the Hebrew word for *dance*, which means "to whirl around." King David was known to dance before the Lord with all his might (2 Sam. 6:14). People may be observed jumping, running, and moving under the power of the Holy Spirit.

Again, Scripture does not specify this is an activity found often in the church, but there is precedent for such happenings. When God touched the disabled legs of the beggar at the temple, the Bible tells us that Peter pulled the man to his feet.

> So he, leaping up, stood and walked and entered the temple with them—walking, leaping, and praising God. And all the people saw him walking and praising God.
>
> —ACTS 3:8–9

We should be careful not to hastily dismiss such bodily manifestations. We cannot always know what circumstances surround the leaping and jumping!

Falling Out in the Spirit

Notice some biblical evidence for this phenomenon. In Genesis 2:21, God caused a "deep sleep" to fall on Adam so He could remove a rib in order to fashion woman. He then closed Adam's side. He performed all of this surgery while Adam slept. He not only removed the rib, but He also healed Adam's body after the surgery. Many have wondered if perhaps Adam had a scar on his side as a reminder that Eve was a gift to him. (We know that the Second Adam had His side ripped open and still bears the scar showing His love to us.) Adam felt God's touch on his life in his physical body.

What God did then, He can do now. During a "falling out" time God can perform surgery and healing for people in a spiritual, emotional, mental, or physical way.

In Genesis 15:12, God put Abram into a deep sleep. God then prophesied or spoke the future over Abram's resting spirit. He told Abram that his descendants would be slaves in Egypt for four hundred years. After that period of bondage, He said Abram's descendants would be delivered and would march out of Egypt with great wealth. Not only did God prophesy the future, but He also promised that Abram would live to a great old age and would be buried with his fathers. Abram listened in his trance and heard the voice of God.

In Numbers 24, God used a mercenary false prophet, a mere magician and sorcerer, to speak the word of God. Balaam had made a deal with Balak, the king of Moab. For big bucks, Balaam agreed to curse the children of Israel publicly. Verses 4 and 16 state of Balaam: "[He] sees the vision of the Almighty, [he] falls down, with eyes wide open."

Each time Balaam tried to curse the people of God, he fell down with his eyes wide open, seeing a vision from Almighty God. Instead of curses, blessings for the nation of Israel came rushing out of his mouth! That happened not once but three times. Angrily, King Balak shouted that the deal was off. Balaam would get no money from him! The fourth time Balaam opened his mouth, he prophesied in verse 17: "A Star shall come out of Jacob; a Scepter shall rise out of Israel."

In a trance, the unbelieving follower of witchcraft saw a vision of God and prophesied the word of God. How amazing to consider that through a trance, God used Balaam's mouth for His glory!

Even today, God can and does turn unbelieving occult followers into preachers of His gospel. Several months ago, a teenager stood in our service and gave testimony to Christ's intervention in her life. She and her friends had become deeply involved in Wicca, or supposed "white" magic. She had soon become dissatisfied with it and began to experiment with more blatant occult practices. She found herself gripped by something she could no longer control, and drug and alcohol abuse added to her problems.

The tormented young lady was put in contact with our deliverance counseling ministry. She was gloriously saved and set free and now gives her testimony to warn others of the dangers of playing around with the lure of power that Satan uses to entangle souls.

The prophet Ezekiel had several experiences in which God visited him in a trance. In Ezekiel 1:28, he described the first of them and recorded his response: "This was the appearance of the likeness of the glory of the LORD. So when I saw it, I fell on my face."

Ezekiel 2:2 reveals that the prophet saw a vision and heard a voice when he fell on his face. The voice commissioned him to a ministry to a rebellious people, and the voice told Ezekiel not to be afraid. While Ezekiel was in a trance, God called him to a new work—a new ministry.

Ezekiel described another supernatural experience:

> The glory of the LORD stood there, like the glory which I saw by the River Chebar; and I fell on my face.
> —EZEKIEL 3:23

During a trance experience, Daniel heard the voice of an angel speaking about the end of time. Daniel 8:27 states that when the trance was over, Daniel fainted and was sick for several days.

Falling Out in the New Testament

The New Testament also records many biblical accounts that support this strange and unusual phenomenon labeled "falling out." The first reference is Matthew 17:1–6, which is an account of the Transfiguration. On the mountain, God showed three disciples what the significance of the Law and Prophets was and that Jesus was greater and the fulfillment of both. When the disciples heard that, they fell to the ground with faces down. They were terrified and totally overwhelmed by both the words of the revelation and the way it was delivered. Jesus touched them and reassured them gently.

The account in Matthew 28:4 tells us that the soldiers who were guarding Jesus's tomb were literally paralyzed with fear when the angel appeared sitting on the stone that was rolled away. The guards were so afraid of the angel that they "shook for fear of him, and became like dead men." Their fear (reverence) in the presence of the angel made them fall as though they were slain. Notice that in the presence of God's power, both believers and unbelievers seem to be unable to stand.

The Book of John tells the account of unbelievers falling in the presence of something holy. In this account Judas and the Roman soldiers had come to arrest Jesus. Jesus identified Himself, saying, "I am He" or "I AM." The power in His words caused the soldiers to move away from Jesus, and then they suddenly fell to the ground (John 18:1–6).

In the Book of Acts, the apostle Paul recorded two separate visitations from God. The first encounter took place as he was on the road to Damascus with papers to arrest more Christians. Paul (or Saul, as he was known before his salvation) was responsible for the deaths of many believers. In Acts 9:3, a blinding light from heaven appeared and seized Saul. He heard a voice from heaven and fell to the ground blinded. His fellow travelers also heard the voice but saw nothing except Saul's response and blindness: "Then he fell to the ground, and heard a voice saying to him, 'Saul, Saul, why are you persecuting Me?' And he said, 'Who are You, Lord?' And the Lord said, 'I am Jesus, whom you are persecuting'" (Acts 9:4–5). Here again we see clear evidence of falling out as a natural response to a divine revelation.

Paul arose from that experience blinded for several days. Although his physical sight was temporarily gone, his spiritual eyes could see clearly. In a trance, he received confrontation and correction from Jesus. Paul recounted this experience before the Jews in Jerusalem in Acts 22 and again before King Agrippa in Acts 26.

Another encounter experienced by Paul is recorded in Acts

22:17–18: "Now it happened, when I [Paul] returned to Jerusalem and was praying in the temple, that I was in a trance and saw Him [Jesus] saying to me, 'Make haste and get out of Jerusalem quickly, for they will not receive your testimony concerning Me.'"

Paul definitely heard the voice of Jesus while he was in a trance. We do not know whether or not he had fallen to the ground, but he was out of consciousness and totally absorbed or engaged in communion with Christ. The purpose of the trance was to give Paul deliverance from his enemies. The experience happened to him in church. God needed to give Paul specific instructions, for more than forty Jewish leaders had sworn an oath that they would neither eat nor drink until they had killed Paul. God supernaturally revealed that He had other plans for Paul!

Acts 10:10–17 records yet another apostle's experience. Peter had gone out onto a housetop to pray while his hosts were preparing dinner. There he "fell into a trance." In the vision, Peter saw a sheet let down from heaven with all kinds of animals on it. The voice in the vision said, "Rise, Peter; kill and eat." Peter responded by saying, "Not so, Lord! For I have never eaten anything common or unclean." The voice rebuked Peter, saying that what God had cleansed, he should never call common. The exchange happened three times. God used the vision to call Peter to minister to a man named Cornelius in Caesarea. God was making Peter ready for a new ministry to the Gentiles. Peter heeded the vision that called him to a new task.

The whole Book of Revelation is a vision of God's glory to the beloved apostle John. Revelation 1:1 gives this introduction to the book: "The Revelation of Jesus Christ, which God gave Him to show His servants—things which must shortly take place. And He sent and signified it by His angel to His servant John." Verse 10 gives further details when John says, "I was in the Spirit on the Lord's Day, and I heard behind me a loud voice, as of a trumpet." But Revelation 1:17 gives us a compelling piece of information: "And when I saw Him, *I fell at His feet as dead.* But He laid His right hand on me, saying to me, 'Do not be afraid; I am the First and the Last'" (emphasis added).

John in his vision saw many things and heard the voice of Jesus. He was a witness to the Word of God and a witness to the testimony of Jesus. He saw, heard, and obeyed the heavenly vision.

Notes From History

Here again are the great revivalists from history who observed instances of resting in the Lord.

Jonathan Edwards, the main instrument and theologian of the Great Awakening in America (1725–1760), said in his *Account of the Revival of Religion in North Hampton in 1740–42:*

> ...many in their religious affections being raised far beyond what they had ever had before: and there were some instances of persons lying in a sort of trance, remaining perhaps for a whole twenty-four hours motionless, and with their senses locked up; but in the meantime under strong imaginations, as though they went to heaven, and had there a vision of glorious and delightful objects.[5]

Charles Finney (1792–1875) was one of the most powerful revivalists since the Reformation. At a country place named Sodom, in the state of New York, Finney gave one address in which he described the condition of Sodom before God destroyed it:

> I had not spoken to them in this strain of direct application, I should think, more than a quarter of an hour, when all at once an awful solemnity seemed to settle down upon them; the congregation began to fall from their seats in every direction, and cried for mercy. If I had had a sword in each hand, I could not have cut them off their seats as fast as they fell. Indeed nearly the whole congregation were either on their knees or prostrate, I should think, in less than two minutes from this first shock that fell upon them. Every one prayed for himself, who was able to speak at all.[6]

What does God do when you fall out in a trance? God does exactly what He wants to do. His ways are not our ways, but we know that He does all things well! In every case, Jesus accomplishes a deeper work in the believer. He may perform surgery; heal your body; prophesy; give a promise; speak a strange word out of your mouth; send an angel; give instruction, correction, or deliverance; or call you to a new ministry. Whatever He does is communication from the Spirit of God to the spirit of man—Spirit-to-spirit contact. This bypasses your mind, will, emotions, thoughts, carnal desires, limitations, and demonic strongholds.

I like to think of falling out as a time-out with the Lord. If you are a parent, you may be familiar with that term. Little children are often placed in a time-out corner or chair in order to think about what they have done or failed to do. They are isolated from a group to calm their busy little bodies.

In the same way, we may need a time-out from our busyness. Our heavenly coach may choose to take us out of the game temporarily. He may pull us aside to say a word of praise for a job well done. Our heavenly coach may need to say, "Come away and rest awhile!" He may have a new play or assignment for us, or He may change the game plan altogether. The Father may sense that we are hurt and need time for healing. Whatever the reason for a time-out with our heavenly coach, we must listen to Him and trust Him, for it will always be for our own good.

Purposes for Manifestations

Manifestations are often responses to the Lord's presence. At other times God uses manifestations to break our pride. Our flesh does not want to be humbled or exposed before others. God can also use the unusual happenings to expose religious traditionalism and its bondage. God may offend the flesh in order to expose a proud heart.

In some instances God's plan may be to declare the sovereignty of His Holy Spirit through supernatural manifestations. Jesus warned Nicodemus that the Holy Spirit cannot be contained or controlled by the flesh. God desires for us to be continuously filled with the Holy Spirit. It pleases Him to bring upon us fresh anointing and revelation of His presence.

How Can We Be Sure These Things Are Real?

As you see manifestations, you know that they must be coming from somewhere. Unfortunately, they sometimes are a person's own emotional response. On some occasions, they may even be demonic. Other times, people may be imitating one another. But you always must consider that what you see could be a genuine work of the Holy Spirit.

The truth is, you cannot always know. As human beings, we cannot unfailingly discern the spiritual condition of another heart. It is true that in every revival through the ages, manifestations have occurred that were strictly emotional acts and demonic imitations.

Why would Satan counterfeit these experiences? Consider this: Counterfeiters always make copies of something valuable! Satan loves to counterfeit true biblical experiences in order to discredit the work of God. Second Corinthians 11:14 warns us, "Satan himself transforms himself into an angel of light."

Even though we cannot know for sure, we can test the manifestations in the following ways.

The word test

Ask, "Does what I see have biblical precedent? What principles of Scripture support these actions?" The early Christians knew the importance of this: "These were more fair-minded than those in Thessalonica, in that they received the word with all readiness, and searched the Scriptures daily to find out whether these things were so" (Acts 17:11).

The warfare test

The church should test the Spirit in a person:

> Beloved, do not believe every spirit, but test the spirits, whether they are of God; because many false prophets have gone out into the world. By this you know the Spirit of God: Every spirit that confesses that Jesus Christ has come in the flesh is of God, and every spirit that does not confess that Jesus Christ has come in the flesh is not of God. And this is the spirit of the Antichrist, which

you have heard was coming, and is now already in the world.

—1 JOHN 4:1–3

Leaders should ask the persons in whom there is a tongue, a sign, or a manifestation to confess by the Spirit controlling them that Jesus is Lord. If they cannot, then they likely are trafficking with a demon. Pastors and leaders must exercise discernment and rebuke those who are not of the Spirit.

The works test

What has the manifestation or sign done for the believer or for the church? Has the sign or manifestation become an end unto itself? The signs are never the destination. The real test of the Spirit's work will be clearly displayed in a deeper love for Jesus, a new hunger for Scripture, a passion for lost souls, a thirst for righteousness, and a new love for others.

What Is Divine Order?

In 1 Corinthians 14:40 we read, "Let all things be done decently and in order." God's order may not be our order. Our lives are so out of order that we need to be certain that we are able to judge properly what order is. What God has decreed as order may not be what we consider comfortable. Our ideas of order may be nothing less than weak attempts to control our own spiritual lives, unconsciously leaving God out of the loop.

In 1 Chronicles 13 when David was bringing up the ark to Jerusalem, he failed to do it according to God's instructions. Consequently, a man was killed. Later in 1 Chronicles 15:13, David was careful to observe the correct "order":

> For because you did not do it the First time, the LORD
> our God broke out against us, because we did not con-
> sult Him about the proper order.

When David practiced obedience, the outcome was dra-
matically different. God's order didn't restrict his expression
in worship, for a mass choir, an orchestra, sacrifices, shouting,
and dancing before the Lord accompanied the ark. That was
massive freedom! David knew that he was to love God with
all his heart, soul, mind, and strength, but he was to do so in
obedience to the accompanying instructions.

God continues to expect us to obey and to heed His order.
Acts 5 tells the tragic story of a couple who lied to the Holy
Spirit, not fulfilling their responsibility in giving to God. Ananias and Sapphira pretended they were on the right track;
they at least brought a portion of their tithe to the church. But
because they lied to the Holy Spirit, they were out of order,
and death was the result.

Let us not ignore the instructions of God and the prompting
of the Holy Spirit as we seek to exercise His gifts and function
in the church. It is all about obedience.

Proper Responses to Manifestations

As you examine manifestations in the church, it is important
to ask searching questions:

- Is God leading your leaders? If so, then trust your
  spiritual leaders and open your heart to God.

- Are you afraid of what you don't understand?
  Just because you don't understand it does not
  mean it's not of God.

+ Are you causing problems by your own stand on these issues? These things can become divisive. Be sure that you are not divisive. Don't expect everyone to accept your experience or to repeat it. If you have not expressed certain manifestations, don't judge others who have. Let God be God!

+ Are you open to what God may be doing in others? Even if you don't agree, love them.

What you receive from God will always be good for you and the church. Remember what Jesus said:

> I say to you, ask, and it will be given to you; seek, and you will find; knock, and it will be opened to you. For everyone who asks receives, and he who seeks finds, and to him who knocks it will be opened. If a son asks for bread from any father among you, will he give him a stone? Or if he asks for a fish, will he give him a serpent instead of a fish? Or if he asks for an egg, will he offer him a scorpion? If you then, being evil, know how to give good gifts to your children, how much more will your heavenly Father give the Holy Spirit to those who ask Him!
>
> —LUKE 11:9–13

God will give you good gifts to bless you and the kingdom!

CHAPTER NINE

Seven Dangerous Sins Against the Holy Spirit

THERE ARE SEVEN dangerous sins against the Holy Spirit. All of these sins release awful consequences.

1. *Blasphemy against the Holy Spirit.* The word *blaspheme* means to speak disparaging of and to speak in an insulting way. Those who speak this way insult the Holy Spirit and are doomed forever! (See Matthew 12:31; Hebrews 10:29.)

2. *Lying to the Holy Spirit.* Ananias and Sapphira made a pledge to the church that they did not perform. This cost them their lives. (See Acts 5:3; 8.)

3. *Testing the Holy Spirit.* This third sin is related to Sapphira. Peter speaks to her about "testing" the Holy Spirit (Acts 5:9). The word *test* is *peirazo* in Greek, and it means "to scrutinize." Its root word means "to experiment." Strangely, the English word *piracy* would come from this word. Ananias and Sapphira were trying to "pirate" what belonged to God.

4. *Trafficking the Holy Spirit.* This sin is very similar to the third and is related to the sorcerer Simon found in Acts 8:18–20. Simon thought

he could traffic with the Holy Spirit for money! The Holy Spirit cannot be bought or sold!

5. *Resisting the Holy Spirit.* Stephen charged the religious leaders of his day with this sin in Acts 7:51. Religion still resists the fresh work of the Spirit. (See Ephesians 4:30.)

6. *Grieving of the Holy Spirit.* The Holy Spirit can be put to grief. He is grieved when believers cannot forgive each other and operate in unity (Eph. 4:31–32). The tragic result of grieving the Holy Spirit is having God fight against you. In Isaiah 63:10, God became the enemy of those who cause His Holy Spirit to grieve.

7. *Quenching the Holy Spirit.* This is where I want to focus in more detail. Paul had several brief exhortations for the Thessalonian Christians, and we find one of those recorded in 1 Thessalonians 5:19: "Do not quench the Spirit." It is interesting to see how different English translations and paraphrases treat this verse: "Quench not the Spirit" (KJV). "Do not put out the Spirit's fire" (NIV). "Do not smother the Holy Spirit" (TLB).

The word *quench* translates from a Greek word that means "to extinguish a flame" or "to suppress or stifle." Its tense in the original language could better be translated, "Do not ever put out the fire of the Holy Spirit." It requires continuous action and is a continuing command.

The following verse indicates that some held the prophetic word given by the Spirit in the church to be contemptible.

They despised what happened that was out of their control: "Do not despise prophecies" (1 Thess. 5:20).

You see, it is possible to throw cold water on someone else's passion for Christ. We are told that never, under any circumstance, are we to suppress the genuine work of the Holy Spirit.

A Fire Put Out

Years ago at a summer youth camp, a mighty outpouring of God marked an entire week, but the aftermath proved to be a spiritual battle.

After we returned from the camp, our association of churches began to hold monthly youth rallies. The Saturday night events often lasted several hours into the night, and lives were being profoundly touched. However, adults soon began to complain. They felt the kids were getting "too Christian." Their enthusiasm was spilling over into churches that were used to quieter, orderly services. Before long the legalists prevailed, and the meetings were taken over by "old guard" leadership. The fire quickly burned out.

A few months later, the same parents who complained about the late-night youth meetings were hosting all-night prom parties for their kids, some even including beer drinking. How sad it was to have watched the fires of passion for Jesus quenched by the tepid waters of tradition!

How Does One Quench the Spirit?

First, you may quench the Spirit by ignoring the things of God. A fire left unattended will soon go out. You must personally give attention to the things of the Spirit if your passion is to stay alive. Almost anything alive will die from lack of attention. You must be proactive toward the Holy Spirit.

The Spirit may be quenched by someone else's influence in your life. You've probably come to realize that certain folks tend to be spiritual fire extinguishers. Critical people quench the Spirit of God. Their words, like sharp icicles, freeze out the fire of revival in a heart.

In addition, people with a spirit of performance may quench the Spirit. When there are manifestations of the Holy Spirit, some persons may try to imitate in the flesh or through emotion what the Spirit is doing. The service then loses its focus or becomes a parade of flesh. The Spirit of God is then quenched.

Satan, if given place, can certainly quench the Spirit. He may show up as a critic, but more often than not he will show up as a counterfeit. Second Corinthians 11:14 reminds us, "And no wonder! For Satan himself transforms himself into an angel of light."

Satan's demons may move someone to show a false manifestation. In this way, confusion is sown and the Holy Spirit quenched. At one time a man who attended our church would shout aloud at inappropriate times in a service, often disrupting a soloist or interrupting the preaching. He was called in for loving correction, but he reacted with extreme hostility and left the church. Several years later we discovered that he was the master of an occult fraternity.

It is very common for fear to quench the Spirit of God. In the first chapter of Paul's second letter to Timothy we see the cruel work of the spirit of fear:

> Therefore I remind you to stir up the gift of God which is in you through the laying on of my hands; for God has not given us a spirit of fear, but of power and of love and of a sound mind.
>
> —2 Timothy 1:6–7

Paul reminded the young pastor to "stir up the gift of God." This could be translated as "fan the flame of the *charisma*, which is in you." Fear had tried to rob Timothy of power, love, and a sound mind. We should not allow the spirit of fear or timidity to put out the fire of God's charisma given to us all.

Of course, a departure from the Bible can quench the Spirit. True worship will strike a balance between the divine Word and the divine wind of the Spirit.

Both truth and Spirit are needed for God's power to be unleashed:

> But the hour is coming, and now is, when the true worshipers will worship the Father in spirit and truth; for the Father is seeking such to worship Him. God is Spirit, and those who worship Him must worship in spirit and truth.
>
> —JOHN 4:23–24

An unwillingness to change can quench the Spirit of God. Methods and tradition can become confused with Scripture. Listen to Jesus's warning in Matthew 15:9: "In vain they worship Me, teaching as doctrines the commandments of men." The Living Bible states it this way: "Their worship is worthless, for they teach their man-made laws instead of those from God."

When we get stuck in the past and long for the way it used to be before God's power fell, then we strip the Word of its miracle-working power. When we dull the blade of the two-edged sword with old traditions, the Word can no longer pierce as deeply into our hearts.

How to Rekindle the Flame

To restore lost power, you must fall in love with Jesus again. Rejoice again at His birth! Thrill again at His power! Weep at His crucifixion! Shout over His resurrection! Live expecting His return! Furthermore, hang out with Spirit-filled people. Stay around people who encourage you. Negative people will pull you down.

You should strive for a Bible-based, praise-saturated, and prayer-empowered lifestyle. Make your home a place where God is worshiped. As you drive to work or school, fill your car with praise music and Bible teaching.

In addition, go to a church that is moving with the Spirit of God, even if it doesn't carry your label. Don't expect a church to change to suit you. If you have waited and prayed for several years and it still seems like an ice rink (people going in circles within a frozen atmosphere!), go to a place where you feel God is at work.

It is important to learn to live and give by faith. Faith brings the wonder back to the Christian life. Learn to hear God, and trust Him for resources. Learn to be a channel of blessing to others.

Finally, find an outlet of ministry through which you can serve others. Discover your spiritual gifts, and go for it in the name of Jesus. Reach out to the lost, helpless, hurting, and homeless. Touch someone else with the fire of God in your life, and rather than quench the flame of the Spirit, you will watch it spread like wildfire.

CHAPTER TEN
Traditionalism vs. Real Biblical Truth

THE WORK OF the Holy Spirit must always be grounded in biblical revelation. This does not mean that the church must be bound to religious traditionalism. Jaroslav Pelikan has said, "Tradition is the living faith of those now dead while traditionalism is the dead faith of those now living."[1] Tradition says, "Worship on the Lord's day!" Traditionalism says, "It must be at 11:00 a.m. in a building with a steeple and pews."

We must differentiate between human customs and real biblical truth. Also we must be careful not to press human, denominational, or other parameters onto Scripture.

The most difficult task for individual Christians and churches is to embrace change. Though God never changes, human beings must change. The whole concept of repentance reflects this truth. The word *repent*, *metanoia* in Greek, means to change one's thinking!

Proverbs 14:4 makes a practical observation of life: "Where no oxen are, the trough is clean; but much increase comes by the strength of an ox." You see, oxen mess up the barn, but that was the high cost the Old Testament farmer had to pay in order to have animals available to help in planting and harvesting.

Revival and growth are often messy. We should keep in mind this proverb and remember that where there is life, there will be evidence of life, and life can make things messy.

When Jesus inaugurated His Spirit-anointed ministry in His hometown of Nazareth, He challenged the status quo. In Luke 4:16–30, Jesus messed up the religious barn. He exposed an attitude that I call "the Nazareth mentality." Speaking in His home church in Nazareth, He selected Isaiah 61:1–2 for His text:

> The Spirit of the Lord GOD is upon Me, because the LORD has anointed Me to preach good tidings to the poor; He has sent Me to heal the brokenhearted, to proclaim liberty to the captives, and the opening of the prison to those who are bound; to proclaim the acceptable year of the LORD.

While acknowledging the power of Jesus's words, the men of His community had rejected His supernatural claims. This process of thinking has survived in our church to this day. All was well in the synagogue service that day until Jesus closed the Scripture and said, "Today this Scripture is fulfilled in your hearing" (Luke 4:21).

Resisting the Miraculous

The first mark of this Nazareth mentality is that people operate as though the Word of God is either for the past or for the future. However, the members of this generation do not want a new word; they want a *now* word. They want the word applied to their lives. Unfortunately, those who maintain the Nazareth mentality love to talk about the miracles of the Bible or the great things that will happen in the future, but they resist the thought of any of those things happening today.

Why do some resist the thought of signs and wonders occurring in today's world? I know many friends who believe God is able to do a miracle in our day but don't feel He has done one in recent times. I sense that many of them fear that if they embrace miraculous events such as healing, supernatural provision, and protection, they must embrace other "untidy" things, such as casting out demons or raising the dead. They resist the thought of losing control of the typical order of events in their lives.

Avoiding the Outsider

Second, people with the Nazareth mentality don't want much to do with people who are not "like us." If others don't share our racial, denominational, cultural, or social background, they often disturb us.

When Jesus spoke a now word, it caused an uprising. He knew that throughout biblical history, men had difficulty in accepting ministry that was unusual, and He pointed that out.

> Then He said, "Assuredly, I say to you, no prophet is accepted in his own country. But I tell you truly, many widows were in Israel in the days of Elijah, when the heaven was shut up three years and six months, and there was a great famine throughout all the land; but to none of them was Elijah sent except to Zarephath, in the region of Sidon, to a woman who was a widow. And many lepers were in Israel in the time of Elisha the prophet, and none of them was cleansed except Naaman the Syrian."
>
> —Luke 4:24–27

When Jesus finished speaking those words, the crowd was "filled with wrath" and proceeded to try to throw Him off a cliff! The people wanted nothing to do with the idea that God might want to reach beyond the borders of their comfort zone to do His ministry.

In much the same way, when a minister begins to believe that God can still move today, cross-cultural ministry should happen in our churches, miracles can take place in our day, and the sign gifts are still valid, often his ministry becomes dangerous to the status quo. He may not be brought to the edge of a cliff by an angry mob, but many pastors have lost their church positions as a result of their belief in the power and gifts of the Holy Spirit for today.

Discrediting the Obvious

A third mark of the Nazareth mentality is that it would rather investigate than celebrate the works of Jesus. The Nazareth folk questioned the origin of Jesus and were offended by His claims:

> Now it came to pass, when Jesus had finished these parables that He departed from there. When He had come to His own country, He taught them in their synagogue, so that they were astonished and said, "Where did this Man get this wisdom and these mighty works? Is this not the carpenter's son? Is not His mother called Mary? And His brothers James, Joses, Simon, and Judas? And His sisters, are they not all with us? Where then did this Man get all these things?" So they were offended at Him. But Jesus said to them, "A prophet is not without honor except in his own country and in his own house." Now He did not do many mighty works there because of their unbelief.
> —MATTHEW 13:53–58

When God begins to move, there exists a group that insists on investigating every act of God in order to discredit the supernatural.

In John 9, the man born blind was miraculously healed. He stood before the Pharisees with clear, healthy eyes, and yet the Pharisees rejected the obvious. With the miracle staring them in their faces, they could not accept it because it cut across their legalistic mentality.

Denying the Truth

Last, this mentality reduces Jesus instead of reverencing Jesus. In Luke 4:22, the people in Nazareth called Him "Joseph's son." It is safe to assume that rumors of Jesus's virgin birth had spread throughout Nazareth and the neighboring areas. However, leaning back on their human understanding, they didn't acknowledge it as a supernatural birth, as John recorded in his Gospel. The Nazareth mentality had spread to Jerusalem, for when Jesus was discussing their sin problem with them, they responded:

> "We were not born of fornication; we have one Father—God." Jesus replied, "If God were your Father, you would love Me, for I proceeded forth and came from God; nor have I come of Myself, but He sent Me."
>
> —JOHN 8:41–42

Today the same mentality denies Jesus's supernatural work through His new body, the church. Miracles, signs, and wonders are still offenses to religion. The Jesus of many churches is minimized in size and effectiveness.

Churches that determine to serve a living, powerful Jesus will grow. A church enlarges its ministry through faith in Jesus. How big is Jesus in your church? Oh, how much we need the real, full-size Jesus in our church today!

Waving "Bye" to Jesus

As we study the Gospels, we find that Jesus's works were thwarted, and He chose to move on from Nazareth. Even today He will not stay in an atmosphere of restrictive, prejudicial, religious legalism. Jesus will move on to a people of faith if we reject His work.

Some years ago while attending a conference, I listened to Leonard Sweet, futurist and dean of theology at Drew University, tell of his dreams for a future church that communicates powerfully to today's world. He told how he felt we were currently trying to minister to the world that we wish we had rather than the one we actually have. Sweet called for a church of Spirit-driven leaders who dare to be "dangerously Christian." I recall his words of warning to mainline evangelicals about our work, expressing his fear that churches are not getting "fresh water" from the spiritual wells anymore. He saw the church complacently drawing from the aqueducts of our ancestors, using water that may be stale, even toxic, to today's generation.

We have a whole world out there that is thirsty for the rain. People are hungry for an authentic move of God's power on their lives. The church must be renewed, or our members will go where their needs can be met. We must realize that today's generation longs for a church where the living Jesus is welcomed.

Embracing the baptism of the Holy Spirit is not always welcome. I noticed a resistance in the church immediately. A certain mentality held that everything had to be a certain way according to our tradition. Longstanding church leaders did not know the difference between Scripture and structure, between truth and tradition. I found that almost any person or church "going on" with God was facing opposition. If laypersons would look at their church records, they would see that a strong majority of evangelical churches are declining in growth, giving, attendance, and baptisms.

The reason for this death in church ministry is irrelevant to many people. Too many churches are locked in a 1950s' mentality and refuse to change to meet the needs of this generation. The average church does not want to move out of its comfort zone to touch today's world. Churches must take down their DO NOT DISTURB signs if they expect to survive.

CHAPTER ELEVEN

The Hope for the Church

As the church confronts an increasingly hostile and secular culture, its hope is not another carnal "restructuring." Its hope does not lie in becoming so concerned with relevant communication that it loses its soul. Yes, we must embrace every contemporary way of communicating, but not without the Spirit's approval and enabling. The hope for the church must begin with a total commitment to all of the Scripture, including its miraculous and supernatural endowments. Gideon asked a question that the contemporary church must answer:

> O my lord, if the Lord is with us, why then has all this happened to us? And where are all His miracles which our fathers told us about, saying, 'Did not the LORD bring us up from Egypt?' But now the LORD has forsaken us and delivered us into the hands of the Midianites.
> —JUDGES 6:13, EMPHASIS ADDED

The church must ask that question and then know that the answer is affirmative. For that to happen, we must confront the heresy of cessationism.

Truth vs. Experience

The evangelical world today divides doctrine into two camps, calling its own doctrine "truth based" and calling charismatic doctrine "experience based." There are several problems with this division.

First, there can be no valid Christian doctrine without experience. Scripture was not dictated to a scholar sitting in an office. Scripture was the inerrant, Holy Spirit–inspired witness of men to the mighty acts of God! Some passages of Scripture actually came through the ministry of angels. Other passages were given to men while they were in an ecstatic state. As we saw in an earlier chapter, even the apostle Paul's life was changed not by having an encounter with scholarship, but by being knocked down by the Holy Spirit. We must remember that Jesus spoke of a balance in life, a need to operate in Spirit and in truth.

Second, the Scriptures themselves validate personal encounters with Jesus Christ and the Holy Spirit. Without a doubt the Bible speaks of and encourages personal encounters with God. For many Christians, the Bible has become an icon or an idol. In their error, the Book becomes larger than its Author. The pathway to Christ becomes a destination of its own. Deep Bible study replaces the vital experience of knowing Christ.

Paul felt that salvation was just like a resurrection. He wrote, "And you He made alive, who were dead in trespasses and sins" (Eph. 2:1). To Paul, the goal of the Christian life was not greater knowledge of the Hebrew Old Testament, his Bible. The goal was to know Christ: "That I may know Him and the power of His resurrection, and the fellowship of His sufferings, being conformed to His death" (Phil. 3:10).

Third, evangelical tradition and theories are often lifted higher than Scripture. One such tradition is cessationism, which teaches that all of the miracles and supernatural gifts ceased sometime during the early church age. One aspect of this belief argues that the gifts were uniquely given for a time to fulfill the promise given in Acts 1:8. At that time, the apostles were promised power as they ministered in "Jerusalem, and in all Judea and Samaria, and to the end of the earth." Some hold the argument that once tongues were revealed in each of these places, they were retracted, and the promise was fulfilled. However, there remain parts of our world that do not know the gospel, so how could this promise be completed?

Others who hold to cessationism argue that the gifts ceased when the last apostle died. Mark 16:17–18 contradicts this belief because Jesus promised that signs and wonders would follow "those who believe." Still others insist the gifts came to an end when the canon of Scripture was completed. Unfortunately, they cannot cite an exact date for this occurrence, since there is much debate about when the canon was actually closed, and argument continues about the Apocrypha, which some insist should have been included in our Bible.

Yet another separate theory called dispensationalism concerns the dividing of Scripture into ages. This theory is a man-made system. Furthermore, a theory continues to survive that teaches there are only three periods of miracles in all of history, which we will discuss further in this chapter. All of these theories and ideas are often elevated to the same plane as the Holy Scriptures.

Many people have made the false accusation that our brothers and sisters in the renewal movement base all of their beliefs on experience without the authority of Scripture. This accusation is obviously unfounded when one reads the carefully indexed works of Jack Deere, Jon Mark Ruthven, and other scholars. Their studies are meticulously documented with Scripture.

Were There Only Three Periods of Miracles?

Evangelical embarrassment over the supernatural dates back
to the Reformation. John Calvin, Martin Luther, and Ulrich
Zwingli railed against both the papacy and what is called the
radical reformation. Baptists, Methodists, Church of God,
Assemblies of God, Congregationalists, and others have roots
in this so-called radical reformation. Luther, at best, arranged
the New Testament to fit his theology and, at worst, denied
the biblical authority of the supernatural in much of the New
Testament. He even rated certain books in the New Testament above others. Jon Mark Ruthven cites Luther's "Preface
to the New Testament," in which Luther elevated the Books
of Romans, Galatians, Ephesians, and 1 Peter as "the true and
noblest books." Luther's sole criterion for selecting these books
as superior was that they did not contain any descriptions of
supernatural works or miracles.[1]

Building upon this approach that demeans much of Scripture, evangelical scholars have sectioned off the Bible into
acceptable and unacceptable Scriptures. Unlike the position
of the classic liberal, who denies all the miracles in Scripture,
the trend today is to categorize them as past events. In this
way the "problem" of supernatural manifestations is quietly
disposed of. Historical tradition has robbed today's church of
supernatural power.

The theory of the existence of only three periods of miracles
in the Bible has been popularized in our day by popular Bible
teacher John MacArthur in his book *Charismatic Chaos*.[2] In
MacArthur's view, God performed miracles only in three brief
periods when He was inspiring Scripture. The problem with
this view is that it is totally without biblical support.

According to this theory, miracles happened only from

the period of Moses to Joshua (during the giving of the Law), in the period of Elijah and Elisha (giving us the prophets' writing), and in the period of Christ and the apostles (during the forming of the New Testament).

Author Jack Deere, on the other hand, has pointed to the miracles that took place outside these three special periods of revelation. Deere counters the skeptics by listing the miracles that were performed outside the supposed three periods, the number of which is absolutely overwhelming! Let us take our own walk through the Bible to examine the supernatural events that took place during the "gaps" between the supposed periods of miracles.

Miracles in the Old Testament

After reading some scholars, you would expect to find no miracles outside these three defined periods. All of the weird stuff should be isolated only to these periods and not disturb the rest of history, right?

Wrong! Let's start in Genesis, where we find the following:

+ The miracle of creation (Gen. 1)
+ The rapture of Enoch (Gen. 5:24)
+ The Flood (Gen. 6–8)
+ The Babel experiences (Gen. 11)
+ The call of Abram (Gen. 12:1–3)
+ Abram's trance, the smoking fire pot, and the blazing torch (Gen. 15)
+ An angel appears to Hagar (Gen. 16:7)
+ The destruction of Sodom (Gen. 19)
+ Lot's wife turned into a pillar of salt (Gen. 19)

+ The miraculous birth of Isaac (Gen. 21)
+ The angel preventing Abraham killing Isaac (Gen. 22)

That is only half the Book of Genesis, dating to about 2000 B.C. Let's look at the Old Testament and test the veracity of this three-period theory to see what happens:

+ All of the miracles in the lives of Jacob and Joseph recorded in Genesis are eliminated.
+ All of the miracles in Judges performed by Samson don't count.
+ Hannah's miracle birth of Samuel must go.
+ King Saul's encounter with the Holy Spirit is irrelevant.
+ David's victory over Goliath was just luck.
+ All of the miracles in Daniel are, in fact, not miracles at all.

Do you get the picture? Our miracle-working God does not fit in a man-made theory. His supernatural power explodes across all the pages of Scripture.

Did Miracles Cease With the Apostles?

Those who believe that the miracles and some of the gifts of the Spirit ceased at the death of the last apostle base their theory on these points:

+ Miracles happen purely to validate new doctrine.
+ Miracles happen only at times when God is inspiring Scripture.

+ Those who believe in supernatural power and gifts today are accused of elevating their experiences to a level equal with the inspired Scriptures.

These are false assumptions and accusations.

Where did this idea of the cessation of miracles and gifts arise? Cessationist theories go back to Calvin, Luther, and Zwingli. The Reformers, reacting to the false miracle reports of Roman Catholicism, such as the figure of the Virgin Mary appearing on a wall, as well their fear of the fringe groups such as Anabaptists, launched them to react to the supernatural.

The Reformers and their successors today teach that miracles rarely happen anymore. We must look to theologian B. B. Warfield's *Counterfeit Miracles*, written in response to the rise of Pentecostalism in the early part of this century, as the foundation of today's argument.[3] What Warfield lacked in biblical support, he seemed to make up for with dogmatic assertion of his theories. Warfield accepted that "general supernatural acts" including healing might happen, yet he felt they could not truly be called miracles. He further proceeded to divide "spiritual gifts" into ordinary and extraordinary. Again, that view has no biblical support. Warfield used the same arguments that liberals use when they attack the miracles of the Bible, even as he proceeded to attack those who believe miracles still happen today.

Even more distressing was Warfield's intellectual arrogance, for he stated that "right-thinking" people (or people in their right minds!) would clearly understand that miracles don't happen in this age, as if the natural man could ever perceive the "things of the Spirit." As a matter of fact, Scripture explains why Warfield and many of his fellow theologians could not come to terms with the supernatural: "But the natural man does not receive the things of the Spirit of God, for they are foolishness to him; nor can he know them, because they are spiritually discerned" (1 Cor. 2:14).

Miracles were not given as proofs; rather, they were a revelation of God and His character. Make no mistake; when God's kingdom breaks through today, there will still be supernatural manifestations.

The Bible Annihilates Cessationism

Both 1 Corinthians 1:4–8 and 1 Corinthians 13:8–13 teach that the gifts of the Spirit and the supernatural works of God will continue until the second coming of Jesus Christ. The Holy Spirit is God's promise to every believer:

> Then Peter said to them, "Repent, and let every one of you be baptized in the name of Jesus Christ for the remission of sins; and you shall receive the gift of the Holy Spirit. For the promise is to you and to your children, and to all who are afar off, as many as the Lord our God will call."
>
> —ACTS 2:38–39

The miracle of Pentecost does not need repeating. Yet its promise is mine. Down to this very age, the Holy Spirit's benefits are available to you and me.

As we journey through the Book of Acts, we find verification of the promise of the Spirit. In Acts 8:14–17 the Gentiles received the power of the Holy Spirit.

> Now when the apostles who were at Jerusalem heard that Samaria had received the word of God, they sent Peter and John to them, who, when they had come down, prayed for them that they might receive the Holy

> Spirit. For as yet He had fallen upon none of them. They had only been baptized in the name of the Lord Jesus. Then they laid hands on them, and they received the Holy Spirit.

In Acts 10:44–48, the Gentile household of Cornelius received the Holy Spirit, including a manifestation of tongues, astounding the Jews.

> While Peter was still speaking these words, the Holy Spirit fell upon all those who heard the word. And those of the circumcision who believed were astonished, as many as came with Peter, because the gift of the Holy Spirit had been poured out on the Gentiles also. For they heard them speak with tongues and magnify God. Then Peter answered, "Can anyone forbid water, that these should not be baptized who have received the Holy Spirit just as we have?" And he commanded them to be baptized in the name of the Lord. Then they asked him to stay a few days.

In Acts 15:8–9 and 12, Paul and Barnabas defended their ministry among the Gentiles, basing this defense on the Pentecostal promise.

> "So God, who knows the heart, acknowledged them by giving them the Holy Spirit, just as He did to us, and made no distinction between us and them, purifying their hearts by faith...." Then all the multitude kept silent and listened to Barnabas and Paul declaring how many miracles and wonders God had worked through them among the Gentiles.

In Acts 19:1–7, Paul ministered to some disciples in Ephesus who were previously untaught. They received the Holy Spirit with gifts and a release of supernatural power.

> And it happened, while Apollos was at Corinth, that Paul, having passed through the upper regions, came to Ephesus. And finding some disciples he said to them, "Did you receive the Holy Spirit when you believed?" So they said to him, "We have not so much as heard whether there is a Holy Spirit." And he said to them, "Into what then were you baptized?" So they said, "Into John's baptism." Then Paul said, "John indeed baptized with a baptism of repentance, saying to the people that they should believe on Him who would come after him, that is, on Christ Jesus." When they heard this, they were baptized in the name of the Lord Jesus. And when Paul had laid hands on them, the Holy Spirit came upon them, and they spoke with tongues and prophesied. Now the men were about twelve in all.

And consider Acts 19:11–12:

> Now God worked unusual miracles by the hands of Paul, so that even handkerchiefs or aprons were brought from his body to the sick, and the diseases left them and the evil spirits went out of them.

In Revelation chapter 2, Jesus would chide this church at Ephesus for leaving their first work and first love while remaining orthodox. I believe Jesus was calling them to a return to supernatural power.

Immediately a cessationist will say, "You cannot get doctrine from the Book of Acts!" I find this objection repeatedly mentioned in cessationist literature. To this I respond, "Where does the Scripture say to ignore the Book of Acts for teaching?" The Bible as its own witness says in 2 Timothy 3:16, "All Scripture is given by inspiration of God, and is profitable for doctrine, for reproof, for correction, for instruction in righteousness."

Yes, even the Book of Acts can be used to instruct the church.

A Call to the Church

Finally, let us look at some concluding passages. Paul encouraged the Galatian Christians not to forsake the power of the Spirit for the works of their own flesh.

> O foolish Galatians! Who has bewitched you that you should not obey the truth, before whose eyes Jesus Christ was clearly portrayed among you as crucified? This only I want to learn from you: Did you receive the Spirit by the works of the law, or by the hearing of faith? Are you so foolish? Having begun in the Spirit, are you now being made perfect by the flesh? Have you suffered so many things in vain—if indeed it was in vain? Therefore He who supplies the Spirit to you and works miracles among you, does He do it by the works of the law, or by the hearing of faith?
>
> —GALATIANS 3:1–5

Today we have elevated our fleshly theories above Scripture. In Romans 11:29, Paul declared that the charismatic gifts will not be taken away. "Gifts" here is the Greek *charismata*. In the verse Paul stated, "For the gifts and the calling of God are irrevocable." The Living Bible reveals the same verse in this way: "For God's gifts and his call can never be withdrawn; he will never go back on his promises."

Paul further warned us, "[They have] a form of godliness but deny[ing] its power. And from such people turn away!" (2 Tim. 3:5). The Living Bible paraphrases the thought like this: "They will go to church, yes, but they won't really believe anything they hear. Don't be taken in by people like that." I am convinced that today's church needs all the gifts and power of God. Cessationism at best is an excuse for the church's lack of power and the awful absence of Jesus's presence.

In Paul's teachings on the gifts, each gift had a crucial place in the body: "And the eye cannot say to the hand, 'I have no need of you'; nor again the head to the feet, 'I have no need of you'" (1 Cor. 12:21). Today's cessationist would mutilate the body of Christ by cutting off the supernatural gifts.

Even if there must be disagreement, can there not be tolerance at least among those who hold to the inerrancy of Scripture? Appalling ugliness and intolerance can be viewed on all sides of this controversy. The charismatic teacher of healing, F. F. Bosworth, resigned from his own Assemblies of God denomination because he could not embrace "evidential tongues," the belief that tongues were required at the filling of the Holy Spirit as a proof that it actually took place.[4] Bosworth, who wrote the classic *Christ the Healer*, truly believed in tongues as a gift and a prayer language.[5] Yet he believed the Bible taught that a Christian could be baptized in the Spirit without experiencing tongues. After enduring much criticism and ill will from fellow ministers, this great man took a stand and left his denomination.

Today some evangelical groups want to dismiss from the fellowship people they perceive as charismatic. Recently a large denominational body dismissed two of their most effective missionaries in the Pacific region from their posts following a "manifestation" of supernatural works of the Spirit in their churches. The previous year these same two missionaries had led more than fifteen hundred souls to Christ!

Jesus rebuked the intolerance of His own followers.

> Now John answered Him, saying, "Teacher, we saw someone who does not follow us casting out demons in Your name, and we forbade him because he does not follow us." But Jesus said, "Do not forbid him, for no one who works a miracle in My name can soon afterward speak evil of Me. For he who is not against us is on our side."
>
> —MARK 9:38–40

The war must end between truth and Spirit. A marriage of these two will not bring uniformity, but it will bring an incredibly powerful unity. Jesus is alive today and must be released to do His complete ministry in the church.

Let us always rejoice over the work that God does personally and lovingly in the heart of every Christian who isn't afraid to release His Spirit to work in freedom.

The Church of the Future

The baptism of the Holy Spirit releases miracle power, heals broken relationships, and restores the wonder to our faith. Churches must embrace the Spirit's power to have a future. Here is what such revival could bring. The church of the future must meet this generation where it is. What will be the characteristics of this growing church?

A place where Jesus is welcome

The church will not simply talk about Jesus, but it will also welcome Jesus to do His ministry in power. The Lord Jesus had to return to heaven, but He promised to return again to us through the person of the Holy Spirit. Nothing can take the place of the Holy Spirit's presence in the life of the church. Like Samson, today's churches "shake" themselves as before, yet they do not know that the Lord has departed. (See Judges 16:20.)

As recorded in the Gospels, Jesus walked on the water. He appeared in such a different form that not even His disciples recognized Him. They cried out, "It is a ghost." Often when Jesus manifests Himself in ways the church has not seen before, fear may rise. Yet Peter dared to step out and risk all for this "water-walking Jesus."

Suppose that the disciples grabbed their Bibles, consisting of the thirty-nine books of the Old Testament. They found no record that the Messiah would walk on the water. Then, thumping their Bibles, they rejected Him. It would be probable that their failure to act in faith would cause them to die in the storm.

Jesus will not contradict Scripture, but neither is He confined to Scripture. Where there is no clear verse to tell you how to act, there will always be a principle. Jesus is not confined to the Bible; He releases the Bible's truth for us.

Jesus's ministry is poignantly described in Acts 10:38: "How God anointed Jesus of Nazareth with the Holy Spirit and with power, who went about doing good and healing all who were oppressed by the devil, for God was with Him."

A place where the Great Commission is taken seriously

This church will not confine its witness to its own kind. The church that is to survive must die to itself and its culture. Every wall must come down between classes, races, genders, and denominations. Kingdom work will be the priority. The church will reach from the inner city to the ends of the earth.

A place where worship is real and powerful

People will not be spectators at a performance, but they will be participants who celebrate the presence of Jesus. They may sing, clap, move in rhythm, shout, laugh, or weep before the Lord. They may quietly meditate and participate thoughtfully in the elements of a service, not in mere repetition, but in deep awareness of the presence of the almighty God. Whatever the format of the service, hearts are lifted in true worship and God is exalted.

A place where spiritual gifts abound

The church of the future must release all the gifts of the Spirit. This generation wants spiritual ministry. The sick will be prayed for and the demonized delivered.

A place where spiritual battles are won

The church of the future must be an armory for spiritual soldiers. We must equip all of God's people with the sword of the Spirit and with prayer.

A place where the hurting are sheltered

One of the most hurtful and most difficult problems we are encountering is that of the abused woman. In our own ministry, we have reached out to help many women who have experienced spousal abuse. I feel some of the most devastating abuse is the sexual abuse of young girls by religious parents or family members. Sometimes very legalistic, strict parents are the worst victimizers.

Some time ago I received a message from a very hurt woman who proceeded to complain about our ministry. Then she revealed that her preacher daddy visited her bedroom often until she ran away from home at age sixteen. Though she had become quite successful in life, she still blamed God for her past, and she harbored resentment toward all Christian leaders.

At a pastors' conference in another state, I was ministering at the close of a session when an astounding thing happened. I felt impressed to open the altar to minister to women who had been physically or sexually abused in the past. Immediately the altar was crowded as twenty-three pastors' wives came forward, weeping. Most were under thirty-five years of age. As we ministered freedom and deliverance, most were overcome by the power of the Holy Spirit. God began closing emotional wounds and healing hearts that night.

A place where healing occurs

Many today would challenge the idea that God still heals people who are sick. However, the God who does not change still calls to the diseased and hurting soul, "I am the God that healeth thee!"

I have seen God's miraculous power firsthand not only in my church but also in my life and in the lives of my family members. Several years ago while we were attending a convention meeting, my wife was very ill. She had been suffering from the effects of toxic shock syndrome and was almost too weak to stand, but she insisted on accompanying me to a Gaither concert held in the evening. As an introduction to the next song on the program entitled "It Is Finished," Gloria Gaither began calling out names of those for whom she sensed God was preparing a miracle. She declared, "Mrs. Phillips, it is finished tonight, and you are healed!"

Mrs. Gaither had not met us and did not know anything about Paulette. But as they sang that triumphant song, my wife was instantly healed!

A church that wants to minister in the fullness of the Holy Spirit will follow the biblical mandate to pray for the sick, anoint them with oil, lay hands upon them, and trust God in faith for healing. James admonished us, "Confess your trespasses to one another, and pray for one another, that you may be healed. The effective, fervent prayer of a righteous man avails much" (James 5:16). This verse clearly advises us to first take care of our sin problems and then believe God for healing.

A place where families are safe

The church must become family friendly. Children must be welcomed again into the life of the church. Church schedules must be simplified to give people time to be at home. Church events should promote family participation.

A place where the Bible is released in the lives of people

Many evangelical churches have raised a generation whose notebooks are full but whose hearts are cold. They may have all the answers, but they possess no passion for ministry. They have sound theology but no doxology. They can quote entire sermon outlines but cannot get a word from God. The Jesus they know is trapped in their Bibles, notes, theology, and tradition. The living Christ is often missing in the zeal for religion.

The living Jesus wants to take His Word and use it to help others. Let us preach the good news, drive out devils, heal the sick, and see His kingdom on the earth grow.

The Hope of This Generation

The young people and young adults of today are experience oriented. They plunge headfirst into everything. Woe to the leader who thinks he can do ministry with just the facts.

Members of this generation believe in the supernatural. They are also ungrounded in biblical truth. Therefore they are ripe for capture by a cult. The church must become a heart place as well as a head place. These young people expect to be touched and prayed for. They want to participate in worship. They do not want to be an audience. They are more into relationships than rules.

That was what the ministry of Jesus was all about. Jesus was most interested in connecting with people's hearts. Jesus loved to celebrate. Jesus liked having children around. Jesus liked to touch and be touched.

Reclaiming What Is Yours

Out of a desperate hunger and need in my spirit, God brought me to a new level of spiritual life and then poured out His renewal on my family and church. I continue to cherish the great doctrinal heritage that is mine, but I joyfully and fully embrace the baptism with God's Spirit.

My great hope is that all believers will discover the great variety of opportunity and experience that God has available for them. I don't feel every Christian has to have the same experiences as I did; however, I believe these experiences are valid both biblically and historically.

It is not a new thing—God's gifts have always been there for the claiming. Reach out and experience the abundant life of Holy Spirit fullness. You will never be the same.

CONCLUSION

The Baptism of the Holy Spirit and the End of the Age

God's goals for the church and through the church remain sadly unfulfilled. These, unified with a missional vitality, still await a lagging church.

The ideal church was the last dream of Paul the apostle. He spent his life planning, growing, and nurturing the church. His magnum opus to the church is his letter to the Ephesians. In Ephesians Paul sets forth the church as Christ's body, building, and bride. Furthermore, the church's distinguishing mark was the seal or baptism in the Spirit, as I wrote in an earlier chapter.

This glorious church marked by the baptism in the Spirit has an open portal to the supernatural realm. At least fifteen times the Holy Spirit's work is revealed as necessary in the six brief chapters of this letter.

When I look at the letter to the Ephesians, I am looking at the model for the End Time church. In Ephesians 1:17, the End Time church is endowed with wisdom to confront every situation.

The Holy Spirit gives power for supernatural exploits that surpass human dreams, expectation, and abilities. The church's unity is a mighty work of the Holy Spirit that has to be guarded and cherished. However, the church's greatest danger lies in broken unity that grieves the Spirit. The Holy Spirit is available to fill every believer and make worship come alive.

The church is not powerless but called by the Spirit to a war-footing. The whole armor of God includes "the sword of the Spirit, which is the word of God" (Eph. 6:17).

Also, ministry leadership is not a career; it is a vocation for called persons who are viewed as gifts of the Spirit to the church. (See Ephesians 4:11–12.) Spirit-gifted men and women are viewed as enablers to all believers so that the work of the ministry can get done. The church's task must always be undergirded by teams who understand the power of praying in the Holy Spirit.

The present-day church in the West has not achieved this model. The church Jesus is coming for is a church modeled above. This church has developed strong families that bear witness to God's transforming power (Eph. 5:23–6:4). Instead many of our churches are weak, insipid, legalistic, compromised, divisive, and ineffective. Church growth is largely disgruntled members moving from church to church.

Marital difficulties are as difficult and disturbing in the church as they are in society. Militant Islam marches into our once Christian West with increasing authority. Our passionless theology cannot take on the rising hordes of this false faith. Furthermore, the secular mock our faith, and we seem to have no lasting effect on our government or culture.

Nevertheless, I know that Jesus is not coming for a hag or harlot, but He is coming for a bride, a glorious church. Since I know that Jesus is coming for "a glorious church, not having spot or wrinkle" (Eph. 5:27), something big must happen!

There are going to be two great failures in the church. First there will be a departure, an apostasy (1 Tim. 4:1). There will be an utter failure by some who call themselves the church. The lukewarm church mentioned by Jesus in Revelation 3:14–22 will be the reality! Here is a church, as Paul said, "having a form of godliness, but denying the power thereof" (2 Tim. 3:5, KJV).

Seven times in the Book of Revelation, the church is commanded; "He who has an ear, let him hear what the Spirit says to the churches" (Rev. 2:7, 11, 17, 29; 3:6, 13. 22). Those who have "an ear" are those who have been baptized with the Holy Spirit. As we have learned in this book, those who move in the Spirit are given capacity to receive revelation and wisdom from God. Furthermore, the Holy Spirit has not given up on the church. He is still speaking to us and is simply waiting for us to listen and obey His voice.

The last-day church must gather in supernatural arenas and anointing. The church's worship must open heaven and amplify what God is saying today. In true worship, heaven kisses the earth, and the veil between this world and the next comes down. God is going to shake everything in the last days, but we are challenged to stay firm, listen, claim the promise, and receive and serve the kingdom that is ours.

In Revelation 2–3, we have seen that seven times the church is called to listen to what the Holy Spirit says! To all seven churches, seven times Jesus speaks of overcomers: "To him who overcomes…" (Rev. 2:7, 11, 17, 26; 3:5, 12, 21). The word *overcome* is the same word used in Romans 8:37, which states that we are "more than conquerors." The End Time church is called to conquest! In the face of all the opposition, we must know that the Spirit-baptized church will win!

Yes, there is coming the greatest outpouring of God in history upon all who will welcome the Holy Spirit! God's "one new man" will stand up Jew and Gentile, male and female, old and young, and receive the End Time outpouring of the Spirit.

Pentecost did not end in the first century. The "last days" are now upon us.

The church will be revived, not divided. God will pour out His Spirit, release His gifts, and send the saving message of Jesus's cross to the ends of the earth.

FOR FURTHER READING

Anderson, Neil T. *Victory Over the Darkness*. Ventura, CA: Regal Books, 1990.

Anderson, Neil T. and Elmer L. Towns. *Rivers of Revival*. Ventura, CA: Regal Books, 1997.

Baker, John. *Baptized in One Spirit*. Plainfield, NJ: Logos Books, 1967.

Bevere, John. *Breaking Intimidation*. Lake Mary, FL: Charisma House, 1995, 2006.

Brown, Michael L. *Let No One Deceive You: Confronting The Critics of Revival*. Shippensburg, PA: Destiny Image Publishers, 1997.

Campbell, Wesley. *Welcoming a Visitation of the Holy Spirit*. Lake Mary, FL: Charisma House, 1996.

Carrin, Charles. *Sunrise of David, Sunset of Saul*. Boynton Beach, FL: Charles Carrin Ministries, 1998.

Carroll, J. M. *The Trail of Blood*. Lexington, KY: Ashland Ave. Baptist Church, 1931.

Christenson, Larry. *Speaking in Tongues and Its Significance for the Church*. Minneapolis, MN: Dimension Books, 1968.

Cymbala, Jim. *Fresh Wind, Fresh Fire*. Grand Rapids, MI: Zondervan, 1997.

Dole, Stephen H. *Habitable Planets for Man*, 2nd ed. New York: American Elsevier Publishing Co., 1970.

Edwards, Jonathan. *An Account of the Revival of Religion in North Hampton in 1740–1742*. Lafayette, LA: Huntington House, 1994.

———. *Religious Affections*. Edinburgh: Edinburgh's Banner of Truth Trust, 1746, 1986.

Finney, Charles G. *Memoirs of Rev. Charles G. Finney*. New York: Fleming H. Revell Company, 1876.

Frodsham, Stanley H. *Smith Wigglesworth: Apostle of Faith*. Springfield, MO: Gospel Publishing House, 1997.

Gilbert, L. *How to Find Meaning and Fullfillment Through Understanding the Spiritual Gifts*. Lynchburg, VA: Church Growth Institute, 1987.

Grudem, Wayne A., general editor. *Are Miraculous Gifts for Today?* Grand Rapids, MI: Zondervan, 1996.

Hart, Larry D. *Truth Aflame*, revised edition. Grand Rapids, MI: Zondervan, 1999, 2005.

Jones, R. B. *Rent Heavens: The Welsh Revival of 1904*. Asheville, NC: Revival Literature, 1997.

Kydd, Ronald A. *Charismatic Gifts in the Early Church*. Peabody, MA: Hendrickson Publishing, 1984.

———. *Healing Through the Centuries: Models for Understanding*. Peabody, MA: Hendrickson Publishing, 1998.

Lloyd-Jones, D. Martyn. *God's Ultimate Purpose: An Exposition of Ephesians 1*. Grand Rapids, MI: Banner of Truth, 1986.

McDonnell, Kilian and George T. Montague. *Christian Initiation and Baptism in the Holy Spirit: Evidence From the First Eight Centuries.* Collegeville, MN: The Order of Saint Benedict, Inc., 1991, 1994.

Olford, Stephen F. *The Way of Holiness.* Wheaton, IL: Crossway Books, 1998.

Pelikan, Jaroslav. *The Vindication of Tradition.* New Haven, CT: Yale University Press, 1984.

Pierson, Arthur T. *The Acts of the Holy Spirit.* Harrisburg, PA: Christian Publications, 1980.

Potter, C. Burtt. *Baptists: The Passionate People.* Nashville, TN: Broadman, 1973.

Rice, John R. *The Power of Pentecost and the Fullness of the Spirit.* Nashville, TN: Broadman, 1949.

Riss, Richard. *Images of Revival: Another Wave Rolls In.* Shippensburg, PA: Destiny Image Publishers, 1997.

Robertson, A. T. *Paul the Interpreter of Christ.* Nashville, TN: Broadman, 1921.

Ruthven, Jon M. "Can a Charismatic Theology Be Biblical? Foundations for a Charismatic Theology." Virginia Beach, VA: Regent University School of Divinity. http://www.tffps.org/docs/Foundations%20for%20 a%20Charismatic%20Theology.pdf.

———. "Jesus as Rabbi: A Mimesis Christology: The Charismatic Pattern of Discipleship in the New Testament." Cleveland, TN: Society for Pentecostal Studies, vol. 1, 1998.

———. *On the Cessation of Charismata: The Protestant Polemic on Postbiblical Miracles.* N.p.: Sheffield Academic Press, 1993.

Smith, Gerald, compiler. *The Tozer Pulpit: Ten Messages on the Holy Spirit.* Harrisburg, PA: Christian Publications, 1968.

Stone, Barton and J. Rogers. *The Biography of Elder Barton Stone, Written by Himself.* New York: Arno Press, 1847, reprint 1972.

Taylor, Jack R. *After the Spirit Comes.* Nashville, TN: Broadman, 1974.

Torbet, Robert G. *A History of the Baptists.* Valley Forge, PA: Judson Press, 1965.

Tuttle, Robert G. *The Partakers.* Nashville, TN: Abingdon Press, 1974.

Watkins, Mamie. *The Baptism in the Holy Spirit Made Plain.* Greensburg, PA: Manna Christian Outreach, 1975.

Wood, Arthur S. *And With Fire: Messages on Revival.* Washington, PA: Christian Literature Crusade, 1958.

NOTES

Chapter 1
My Own Story

1. Jack R. Taylor, *The Key to Triumphant Living* (n.p.: Baptist Sunday School Board, 1971).

2. The importance of this cannot be overstated. Just as Moses was directed by his father-in-law, Jethro, to choose helpers, the apostles found deacons to take care of day-to-day activities of the church. These deacons were invaluable to maintaining the state of affairs.

Chapter 3
Entering the Spiritual World

1. M. Woolfson, "The Origin and Evolution of the Solar System," *Astronomy and Geophysics* 41, no 1 (2000).

2. Alessandro Morbidelli, "Origin and Dynamical Evolution of Comets and Their Reservoirs," *CNRS, Observatoire de la Côte d'Azur*, December 9, 2005.

3. Linda T. Elkins-Tanton, *The Sun, Mercury, and Venus* (New York: Chelsea House, 2006), 46.

4. National Aeronautics and Space Administration, "Astronomical Unit (AU)," http://neo.jpl.nasa.gov/glossary/au.html (accessed January 19, 2011).

5. S. H. Dole, *Habitable Planets for Man*, 2nd ed. (New York: American Elsevier Publishing Co., 1970).

6. National Geographic, "Earth's Atmosphere," http://science .nationalgeographic.com/science/earth/earths-atmosphere/ (accessed January 11, 2011).

7. The Physics Factbook, "Area of Earth's Land Surface," edited by Glenn Elert, http://hypertextbook.com/facts/2001/DanielChen .shtml (accessed January 11, 2011).

8. SolarViews.com, "Earth Introduction," http://www .solarviews.com/eng/earth.htm (accessed January 11, 2011).

9. Fraser Cain, "Distance From Earth to Sun," UniverseToday
.com, November 12, 2009, http://www.universetoday.com/44815/
distance-from-earth-to-sun/ (accessed January 11, 2011).

10. The Physics Factbook, "Number of Galaxies in the
Universe," edited by Glenn Elert, http://hypertextbook.com/
facts/1999/TopazMurray.shtml (accessed January 11, 2011).

11. About.com, Space/Astronomy, "Top 10 Closest Stars to Our
Solar System," http://space.about.com/od/stars/tp/closeststars.htm
(accessed January 11, 2011).

12. "Old Time Power" by Charles D. Tillman. Public domain.

Chapter 4
The Seal of God

1. D. Martyn Lloyd-Jones, *God's Ultimate Purpose: An Exposition of Ephesians 1* (Grand Rapids, MI: Banner of Truth, 1986).

2. Ibid., 245.

3. "Oh Holy Spirit," poem by Ruth Johnson, copyright © 2002,
http://www.angelfire.com/tx2/christianpoetry/ohholyspirit.html
(accessed January 11, 2011). Permission requested.

Chapter 5
The Baptism of the Holy Spirit
in the New Testament

1. R. A. Torrey, *The Holy Spirit: Who He Is and What He Does*
(n.p.: Bridge-Logos Publishers, 2008), 107–108.

2. R. A. Torrey, "Why God Used D. L. Moody," in James S.
Bell, ed., *The D. L. Moody Collections* (Chicago: Moody Press,
1997), 116–117.

Chapter 6
The Baptism of the Holy Spirit as Your Inheritance

1. *Rain Man*, directed by Barry Levinson. (1988, n.p.: MGM
Home Entertainment, 2000), DVD.

Chapter 7
God's Endowment for Ministry

1. Larry D. Hart, (1999, 2005). *Truth Aflame*, rev. ed. (Grand Rapids, MI: Zondervan, 1999, 2005), 396–399.

2. Ibid., 397.

3. Ibid., 399.

4. Kilian McDonnell and George T. Montague, G. T. (1991, 1994). *Christian Initiation and Baptism in the Holy Spirit: Evidence From the First Eight Centuries* (Collegeville, MN: The Order of Saint Benedict, Inc., 1991, 1994), 176–178.

5. Ibid.

6. Ibid.

7. Ibid., 178.

8. Ibid., 179.

9. Ibid., 183.

Chapter 8
Physical Manifestations of the
Baptism of the Holy Spirit

1. Barton Warren Stone and J. Rogers, *The Biography of Elder Barton Stone, Written by Himself* (New York: Arno Press, 1847; reprint 1972).

2. Jonathan Edwards, *Religious Affections* (Edinburgh: Edinburgh's Banner of Truth Trust, 1746, 1986).

3. Lloyd-Jones, *God's Ultimate Purpose*, 277–278.

4. Stone and Rogers, *The Biography of Elder Barton Stone, Written by Himself*, 41.

5. As related in Jonathan Edwards, "Temporary Abatement of Religious Attention," in *The Works of Jonathan Edwards*, vol. 1 (Carlisle, PA: Banner of Truth Trust, 1834), viewed at Christian Classics Ethereal Library, http://www.ccel.org/ccel/edwards/works1.i.x.html (accessed January 13, 2011).

6. Charles G. Finney, *Memoirs of Rev. Charles G. Finney* (New York: Fleming H. Revell Company, 1876), 103.

Chapter 10
Traditionalism vs. Real Biblical Truth

1. Jaroslav Pelikan, *The Vindication of Tradition* (New Haven, CT: Yale University Press, 1984), 65.

Chapter 11
The Hope for the Church

1. Jon Ruthven, "What's Right About the Faith Movement," HopeFaithPrayer.com, December 4, 2008, http://hopefaithprayer .com/?page_id=846 (accessed January 14, 2011).

2. John MacArthur, *Charismatic Chaos* (Grand Rapids, MI: Zondervan, 1992).

3. Benjamin B. Warfield, *Counterfeit Miracles* (New York: C. Scribner's, 1918).

4. Roscoe Barnes III, "F. F. Bosworth: A Historical Analysis of the Influential Factors in His Life and Ministry (PhD thesis, University of Pretoria, 2009), 209, http://upetd.up.ac.za/thesis/available/ etd-07302010-165851/unrestricted/04chapters5-6.pdf (accessed January 14, 2011).

5. Ibid., 205.

More Foundational Books
From Ron Phillips

978-1-61638-240-7 / $9.99

Book two in the Foundations on the Holy Spirit explains foundational truths for the Spirit-filled believer and shows how the Holy Spirit works in our lives today.

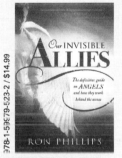

978-1-59979-523-2 / $14.99

The definitive guide on angels and how they work behind the scenes

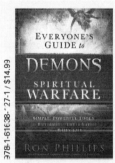

978-1-61638-127-1 / $14.99

Simple, powerful tools for outmaneuvering Satan in your daily life

Available wherever fine Christian books are sold
www.CharismaHouse.com   www.facebook.com/CharismaHouse

CHARISMA HOUSE

9894

FREE NEWSLETTERS
TO HELP EMPOWER YOUR LIFE

Why subscribe today?

❑ **DELIVERED DIRECTLY TO YOU.** All you have to do is open your inbox and read.

❑ **EXCLUSIVE CONTENT.** We cover the news overlooked by the mainstream press.

❑ **STAY CURRENT.** Find the latest court rulings, revivals, and cultural trends.

❑ **UPDATE OTHERS.** Easy to forward to friends and family with the click of your mouse.

CHOOSE THE E-NEWSLETTER THAT INTERESTS YOU MOST:

- Christian news
- Daily devotionals
- Spiritual empowerment
- And much, much more

SIGN UP AT: **http://freenewsletters.charismamag.com**

8178